Advance Praise for Aunt Laya Saul's Book:
You Don't Have to Learn Everything the Hard Way

"Filled with powerful insights, *You Don't Have to Learn Everything the Hard Way* guides and motivates in smart and sensitive ways that any reader can benefit from."
> *–John Gray PhD*
> author of *Men Are from Mars, Women Are from Venus*

"This is a great book that you can give to the teen or pre-teen in your life. Or if you're a young adult looking for a handbook to get through the tough times of adolescence, pick up a copy of *You Don't Have to Learn Everything the Hard Way*. I guarantee you won't be disappointed."
> *–Jennifer Wardrip, TeensReadToo.com*

"I wish a book like this had been available when I was a teen. Every adult should buy a copy for the young person in their lives, and get one for themselves, too. The information is timeless and priceless."
> *–Cynthia Kersey*
> author of *Unstoppable*

"This book is filled with gems and 'A-Ha's!' And it's fun to read! 'Aunt Laya' combines a loving manner, in a non-judging way, with practical advice that will make anyone's life so much easier, and much, much more effective and happy.

As I came across these gems I kept finding myself thinking that if this book was the only one I had known about when I was younger, I could have (and would have) avoided a lot of pain. *You Don't Have to Learn Everything the Hard Way* should be read by every young adult and his or her friends."
> *–Bob Burg*
> author of *Winning Without Intimidation* and
> co-author of *Gossip*

"I found that any teen who is having trouble (and who isn't?) will find this book useful. Plenty of adults can gain from it as well . . . I highly recommend this book to any teenager who would like to feel better about him or her self and even life in general. It will definitely show you a different perspective on life."

> –Yael Sherby for TeenToTeen
> www.ttt.org.co.il

"Laya, We have read your chapter on suicide and are very impressed. You wrote in a manner that kids will keep on reading. Many things that we have seen out there are written over the kids' heads or not to them, but this is right to the point and gets them the information, the resources and the respect that they need and deserve. You've captured the issue and will help their hearts."

> –Dar and Dale Emme
> Yellow Ribbon Suicide Prevention Program®, and
> Light for Life Foundation Int'l
> www.yellowribbon.org

"I think this is a great introduction to the things that 'matter' in a young person's life. We need more resources to help us build character and integrity into this generation. This book speaks directly to the needs of a young man or woman growing up and maturing. Great book."

> –Dale Butler, Youth Pastor,
> Westminster Nazarene Church, Westminster, CO

"I am not quite sure how to express my gratitude and awe towards you and your book. This might not sound very eloquent, but I think that 'WOW' just about sums up the way I feel; it truly is a gift. I have taken so much from your book."

> –Jessica, 18

"Aunt Laya has a way of talking to any person, no matter what age they are in life. This book, as the country song goes, helps me 'to walk on the rocks I stumbled on.' Good book."
　　　–Rachel, 18

"This book made me realize I that I can make my life into whatever I want! It made me think a lot about my life and how I want it to be."
　　　–17-year-old male

"I realized the strongest being is one's self."
　　　–17-year-old female

"It helped me remember it's my life."
　　　–15-year-old male

"If ever there was a 'teen manual' this book is IT! Aunt Laya shares rich life experiences that not only teens will benefit from, but parents will enjoy right along with them. Many of her inspiring lessons took me over forty 'solo' years to discover. This book is so much more than a gift, but a treasure that should not be missed. I sincerely believe Aunt Laya is lovingly changing hearts and minds with the blessings of her book, one teen at a time."
　　　–Kristine L. Joseph, mother of four

You Don't Have to Learn Everything the Hard Way

WHAT I WISH SOMEONE HAD TOLD ME

AUNT LAYA SAUL

Kadima Press, Denver, Colorado
Printed in the United States of America

Cover and book design by Dunn+Associates Design, www.dunn-design.com

Publisher's Cataloging-in-Publication Data

Saul, Laya.
    You don't have to learn everything the hard way: what I wish someone had told me / Aunt Laya Saul. – Rev. ed. – Denver: Kadima Press, ©2008.

    p. ; cm.

    ISBN: 978-0-9723229-7-3
    Includes bibliographical references and index.

        1. Young adults–Life skills guides. 2. Teenagers–Life skills guides.
    3. Preteens–Life skills guides. 4. Life skills–Handbooks, manuals, etc.
    5. Self-actualization (Psychology) I. Title.

BJ1661.S38 2008
646.7/00842–dc22   0801

This book is dedicated to you, the reader, for having the courage to walk the path of growth and for seeking to rise toward your best. May you be blessed as you explore this incredible world. Your own personal answers live within you. Sometimes exploring with others can help you along the way. So, I wrote this book for you with love and high hopes. May you reach for your highest good, the deepest truth, take right action and find joy in so doing.

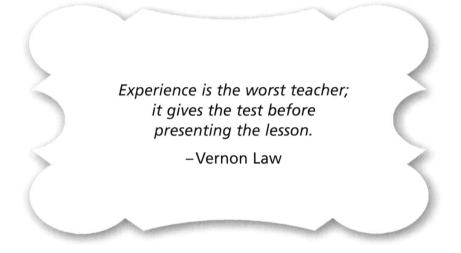

Experience is the worst teacher;
it gives the test before
presenting the lesson.

–Vernon Law

Table of Contents

Dear Nieces and Nephews:
YOU HAVE TO LEARN SOME THINGS THE HARD WAY

"Education is learning
what you didn't even know you didn't know."
–Daniel J. Boorstin

This is the book that I wish someone had written for me. I remember being a teenager and searching for someone who would talk to me about growing into adulthood. If there were books written to address the issues I was struggling with, they never found their way into my hands. The "generation gap" was being promoted: if you were young, the message went, you shouldn't trust anyone over thirty. And yet, those very people had a wealth of life experience that could have saved me a lot of heartache. My problem with the "older" generation was that they had plenty of rules, but no one was talking about why those rules were in place. But I was hungry to know about life. So I looked for answers where I could find them. I reached for popular books and listened to popular songs. And I made a lot of stupid choices. Today I joke that I learned too much "the hard way."

I'm hoping I can pass on to you some of the knowledge I have gained, on my own and from others, in order that your way can be smoother, more joyful, and more fulfilling. I'm hoping to save you a little trouble, or guide you in a way that might shorten the time you spend in the places you don't want to be. At the same time, I hope my words can support you in reaching high and living up to your best potential.

In these pages, I want to encourage you, teach you, laugh with you, and cry with you. I care about how your life goes. I may not know you personally. Or perhaps I do. Either way, I know enough about life to know that we are all connected. Your joy lights up the world. Your pain is part of giving birth to yourself, as it is for us all. I'll hold your hand for a little time, coach you, cheer for you, encourage you. I want to tell you the truth about cause and effect. For each action there is a consequence—nothing personal, it works like that for everyone, even when it doesn't seem to at first glance.

There are laws and rules that exist whether you know about them or not. You may or may not like them. You don't have to believe in gravity or agree with it for this book to fall if you hold it out and let go. As a child, you can be told "HOT!" and it really doesn't mean a thing until you get burned for the first time. After you get a burn and cry, you have a frame of reference for "hot." So, some things you have to learn the hard way. You just do.

You don't, however, need to learn the same things over and over. The interesting thing about life is that you will get knocked on the head as many times as it takes to learn a lesson. Life is a patient teacher that way. This book is about mapping some of the terrain of life and showing you a few places that might be "hot." You decide for yourself how you want to approach things. I hope my words will help you listen to the inner voice you have to guide you and hear it a little more clearly. And I'll whisper some of the things I've learned along the way so you don't have to learn EVERYTHING the hard way. Through sharing stories of my own and other people's lives, I hope to support you in creating the life you dream of, in becoming the best you.

In the world of finance there is a term: OPM. It stands for "other people's money." The idea here is that you can use other people's resources to invest and make a profit for yourself. In this book there is a similar concept for you to use to your advantage. It's also OPM, but here it stands for "other people's mistakes." Where others have shared their life experiences and learned from them, you have an opportunity to benefit. Use other people's mistakes (and successes!) to your advantage.

Making your own mistakes is an essential part of life. Struggling through challenges does make you stronger. Yet knowing that you are not alone in your effort to grow can be enormously encouraging. The journey of life is taking one step at a time. Each new step brings us another chance to grow, strengthen our character, or connect. When you think you have "arrived" at mastery, when you think that you know everything you need to know, that is precisely when life will send you a "wake-up call."

I hope you will see that you are never alone in your experiences, never. There is a paradox here. Because at the same time that you are never alone, you are the only one who can do what you need to do. There are thousands of writers, but I am the only one who can write this book. You are the only one who can make that particular movie, or be a good friend to that particular person in need. A paradox is when two seemingly contradictory things exist at the same time. Even though millions of other people have the same kinds of experiences, each one of us has our own sacred perspective. We each carry a spark of the Divine, and it is that which we honor in our uniqueness. It is also that spark that is always with us no matter how dark life may seem.

We each get to decide for ourselves the kind of life we want. We each have to live our own adventure in life, but we each don't have to reinvent the wheel. Author and teacher Tony Robbins says it very well: "To have good judgment, you have to have life experience. To have life experience, you have to have made bad judgments (and learned from them)."

Experiment for yourself with the concepts presented here. Think of the ideas and life lessons in this book as a cafeteria. You go through and taste different things. You may read out of order or read some chapters more than one time. You may be hungry for certain ideas and find others to be a nice complement for support and balance. Bon appétit!

Love, aunt Jaya

The Butterfly Story

A preschool class was learning about bugs. Everyone got involved in catching, caring for, and watching them. One parent found a butterfly cocoon and carefully snipped the branch it was on so the kids could watch the butterfly emerge. How dramatic it would be in the end to set the butterfly free and watch it fly off into the garden.

When at last the butterfly started to come out of the cocoon, it was a slow process. The teacher was worried that the kids would go home and miss the butterfly finally emerging.

Ever so gently the teacher reached in and helped the butterfly by tearing the cocoon open. The butterfly did crawl out, but beautiful wings did not spread open. The wings were wrinkled and still. The end of the day was near, so the teacher told the kids that tomorrow they would release the butterfly when its wings were ready to fly.

The next day however, they were all disappointed to find that the wings of the butterfly were not ready to fly. It was then that they learned that the struggle to push through the cocoon is what fills the wings and makes them beautiful.

The children learned an amazing lesson that day: struggling in life is necessary. It makes you whole. The teacher learned a lesson, too: letting others work through their own struggles is what really gives them their wings.

Know that the struggles in life make you strong, then take wing, and fly!

Part One

Attitude

"Any fact facing us is not as important
as our attitude toward it, for that determines
our success or failure. The way you think about a fact
may defeat you before you ever do anything about it.
You are overcome by the fact because you *think* you are."

–Norman Vincent Peale

BELIEVE IN YOURSELF

"If I am not for myself, who will be for me?
If I am only for myself, what am I? If not now, when?"

–Hillel

Question: Do you see your own potential?

Do you see a variety of possibilities for living a meaningful life? Your perceptions about yourself—your character, your essence, and the actions you take—will play a big role in what kind of life you are living and where you will find yourself in time. When you line up your perceptions and your actions, you can create the life you dream.

There are going to be times when you doubt yourself, and times when you will be confident. That is natural.

The question is: In what frame of mind do you want to spend the majority of your time? It's your choice.

YOUR UNIQUENESS, YOUR IMPORTANCE

Think of a beautifully cut, faceted gemstone. It is one radiant jewel with many different angles and facets, each reflecting the light in a different way. That's you, unique in this world, hand cut by the master jeweler. No two stones are alike. Even though they may seem the same at first glance, when viewed with a jeweler's loupe and magnified, each has its own size, flaws, and color variations. Sometimes people feel dismay at feeling like just another drone in the masses. Yet, viewed with an open heart and open eyes, each person's uniqueness is revealed. You will see what you look for, so spend your time looking for beauty. How will you polish the stone of your life? How will you set the gem? How can you compare the beauty of one gem against another? Think of a beautiful piece of jewelry with many stones that all seem alike. When one falls out, is the whole not incomplete?

One way this was taught to me was through the analogy of the Hebrew biblical text which is hand written onto a parchment scroll. If even one letter is damaged or missing, the entire text is rendered unusable until the letter is repaired. This is compared to the soul of the individual within the world; each soul is needed to make the world whole.

You hold thx kxy insidx you

Xvxry timx I usx my old computxr—which I lovx— I noticx xvxn though it works rxally wxll in so many ways, thxrx is onx xxcxption. You wouldn't think onx kxy would bx such a big dxal. It sxxms likx such a small pixcx of what makxs up the wholx unit.

It's likx that in lifx, too. Xach onx of us is only onx pxrson. Yxt xach pxrson's xfforts and gifts (and xvxn thxir lovx) makx a big diffxrxncx to this puzzlx of lifx. At homx, at work, xvxn in rxcrxation, who you arx and thx way you arx, makxs a big diffxrxncx.

If you xvxr think that what you do doxsn't mattxr, think of my computxr.

You hold thx kxy and you makx a diffxrxncx!

SELF-PERCEPTIONS

In Buddhist philosophy, there is a term: "monkey mind." This is the part of your mind that is mischievous and troublesome. It chatters away, distracting you from yourself. Maybe it distracts you from meditation, prayer, schoolwork, the task you have at hand to complete, a relationship, or maybe even your heart's dreams and desires. It chatters all of the doubts and it knows them better than anyone because it lives inside you. When you recognize the voice inside you that is "monkey mind," give it a banana, a pat on the head (thanks for the wake-up call), and send it away to play somewhere else. Conquer your doubts, and do what you can.

Take the time to affirm to yourself what you want to be true about you. What are the qualities you admire in others? What you like in others is a reflection of something that already lives inside of you. Claim it as a part of yourself. Make it concrete by writing it down. Then do your best to live up to it.

You are a good person, that is the truth about you. It's good to remember that good people make mistakes. When you find you have made a mistake, do what you can to correct, repair, or heal and go on from there. You are not your mistakes. You are something wonderful, a masterpiece of the Creator.

I have a (yet another) favorite saying: "Anyone who thinks they can't make a difference hasn't been alone in a room with a mosquito." Inside, you know your talents. DO NOT UNDERESTIMATE YOUR STRENGTHS. This is a place to start.

> "Our deepest fear is not that we are inadequate, our deepest fear is that we are powerful beyond measure. It is our light, not our darkness that most frightens us. We ask ourselves, 'Who am I to be brilliant, gorgeous, talented, and fabulous?' Actually, who are you not to be? You are a child of God. Your playing small does not serve the world. There is nothing enlightened about shrinking, so other people will not feel insecure around you. We were born to make manifest the glory of God that is within us. It is not just in some of us: it is in everyone. And, as we let our own light shine, we unconsciously give other people permission to do the same. As we are liberated from our own fear, our presence automatically liberates others."
>
> –Marianne Williamson

Everybody Has Something

"The weakest among us has a gift,
however seemingly trivial, which is peculiar to him,
and which, worthily used,
will be a gift to his race forever."
–John Ruskin

EVERYBODY HAS A CHALLENGE

In our quest to be the best we can be, we have to get real about what we can't do. Nobody does it all, has it all, knows it all. We can feel isolated when we perceive that someone else out there has it together where we don't. Some friends of mine were sitting around one day, discussing their weird quirks and nervous habits. This one bites fingernails, another is a hair-puller . . . this one overeats, that one throws up after eating. One man is compelled to dry his hands in a public restroom with an odd number of towels; if he pulls out an extra one making it an even number, he feels he has to take the extra to make it odd.

Some of these things are harmless and some can be life-threatening. Some things we may have control over, others bring us to the point of risking disease or loss of limb. The main thing to realize is that no matter how weird you think your actions may be, no matter how painful your challenge is, someone else in this world is dealing with, coping with, or healing from the same thing. If your challenge is something that is terribly painful to you, seek help and support. DO NOT ISOLATE YOURSELF: that is the worst thing you can do. Remember, you are not alone.

Some people will just never be good with money. But they could learn how to handle it if it was important enough. Some people will never learn grammar or spelling (hooray for spell-checkers!). Some people will never be thin and some people will never quit smoking. A man came to work in my home for a repair. When he went outside for a smoke break, my young children asked him why he smokes. His reply was, "Because I'm just stupid, I guess." I explained that smart people can make stupid mistakes. This man could quit smoking, if it was important enough to him. It doesn't make him a bad guy!!!

Whatever your habit, compulsion, or challenge, you can change it if you want to. Sometimes people need help and sometimes they don't. If your challenge is harmless to you and others, it's only a problem if it's a problem to you. Of course, this only applies to things that affect no one but you, not things you do that could hurt others. I am not addressing compulsions that involve other people or moral issues. If you are dealing with a behavior that puts you or someone else at risk, you must do what you can to stop. There are support groups for everything these days. There are people who have gotten into the counseling field motivated to help others get through what they themselves have overcome.

While I was working at a residential treatment facility for adolescents, a presenter at an in-service meeting said, "You are here to help other people get through a tough time. Chances are, you had a tough time in adolescence and that's why you're here. You want to help them survive a tough time . . ." It was true for me. Get help if you need it. Asking for help is a way of taking responsibility. Accept yourself with frailties and imperfections. We are all perfectly imperfect. We all have to deal with some challenge.

EVERYBODY HAS A GIFT

What a puzzle this life can be. We come into this world with many of the pieces. But we are missing some of the pieces to our own picture and in their place we have some pieces that fit into other people's puzzles. So we need to go through life giving away the pieces that help others and receiving the pieces that fit for us.

Don't hold back your gift, because you never know when you might be helping someone. We all have a gift to give. Some people seem to have a bigger influence in this world: Mother Theresa, Gandhi, Hillel, the Dali Lama. Some people have a quieter impact, no less important.

My brother is a high school teacher at a school where not every student can afford the high cost of college. He extends himself in ways that go beyond math and believes in every kid that walks into his classroom. Every semester he tells his students, don't worry about paying for college; you set your goals, make the grades, and I'll help you get the scholarships.

The previous owner of a home was a master gardener. He passed away, and although the yard was neglected for a long time, the bulbs he had planted continue to bloom. Each spring, that little corner of the world is lit up with the beauty of his flowers. It is a source of delight for all who see it.

Every preschool teacher invests her love and care into children who may never even remember her name or face! She is concerned with the child each day and takes care to know what's going on in that child's family: did they just move, have a new baby, a divorce, an illness, a growth spurt?

Giving of ourselves, sharing our gift, is what lifts us. The tricky part is, none of us knows exactly how we will impart the gift we have to give: what kind word we speak, what song we sing, which hug we give will be the one that touches another soul. So plant trees, write poems, smile, listen, share yourself, show up. Push yourself to visit a sick or grieving friend. Give an extra coin in the charity box. Tell a story. Play with or read to a child.

One of the wonders in life is when a baby is born. A complete miracle. All a baby has to do is show up and she is loved. I have awaited the birth of many babies, only two of whom were my own, and loved each one before it even arrived. Each of us needs to love and be loved.

Just like every new baby, you are an entire world and you mean the world to someone, even if you don't see that right now. It was true when you were born, and it's true every day. You are a gift just for showing up.

TRUST YOUR INTUITION

"Intuition is similar to a radio receiving set
through which ideas, plans or thoughts flash into the
conscious mind. These flashes have been described as
hunches, inspirations or promptings
of the 'still small voice' within."

—Catherine Ponder

**THERE IS A PLACE INSIDE OF YOU THAT KNOWS.
WE ALL HAVE IT.**
Sometimes it is a nagging, a"gut feeling" that tells you to
change direction. Sometimes it is a sense of peace: things
are, or will be, okay. Among other things your intuition (not
just for women!) might be telling you:

- slow down

- let go

- say NO

- something here is not safe, PAY ATTENTION

YOU DON'T HAVE TO LEARN EVERYTHING THE HARD WAY

- take action NOW
- relax
- something's wrong
- everything will be fine
- BE QUIET, JUST LISTEN

WHERE DOES INTUITION COME FROM?

Intuition comes from a place inside you that connects to a truth that is totally accessible. I've heard people say that intuition is God's voice inside of you, or that it's the voice of an angel whispering in your ear. Even though it seems mysterious in some ways, intuition is like electricity. You flick a light switch on and off and it works even if you don't know anything about the wiring. Plug in to yourself to access your own intuition. Will you be right 100 percent of the time? No. Sometimes our emotions or self doubt will get in the way. We are not prophets, but the more mindful we are about what is going on, the more we will benefit from listening to and following our intuition.

HOW DO YOU "PLUG IN" TO YOUR INTUITION?

Be still. Be silent. Take a deep breath and do not rush. You will learn to recognize thoughts or ideas, the voice of intuition.

Dee was traveling with her toddler son. In the hotel room, she suddenly got the urge to check on him. As she turned the corner, she was just in time to catch the coffee maker complete with a fresh, hot pot of coffee, before it was yanked off the counter onto her curious son.

I once was offered work on a project in a foreign country. I love to travel, and had traveled internationally before, but I had a weird feeling about this one. It felt to me like the sinking feeling you get when you see police lights flashing and you know there's a ticket meant for you! I told the company that the pay wasn't enough, but instead of finding someone else, they offered me more money. Now I really had to face the signals I was getting inside. As hard as it was to turn down the travel and good money, I did exactly that. Several months later, I learned that people died in a helicopter crash during that production. I thought that, knowing the way I jump to try new things, it was likely that I would have been on that helicopter. I'll never know for sure, of course, but hearing that unforgettable news strengthened my trust in my own intuition.

Author Gavin DeBecker, in his book *The Gift of Fear* (highly recommended reading), relates stories of people who would literally have died if they hadn't trusted their intuition, finding the exact opening to escape an attacker, or, sadly, not listening to inner warnings and winding up victims of violent attacks.

Stories are told of people who are suddenly plagued with doubt before they walk down the aisle to marry but do it anyway, ending in divorce shortly thereafter. Because after all, how can we let people down when the invitations have already gone out?

BUT IT'S SO EMBARRASSING!

Sometimes following your intuition can lead to embarrassing behavior. Like walking down the middle of the street during the night so you aren't walking too closely by hidden shadows. Or turning down what looks like a great opportunity.

What's worse, being embarrassed about calling off a wedding or suffering through with the wrong person in a marriage that ultimately ends in divorce? Please don't misunderstand this as an excuse not to marry! It's certainly natural to feel excited or nervous entering into such a serious commitment. The doubt that screams, "Red Flag, red flag, don't do this!" is the one I'm talking about.

TRUST YOUR INSTINCTS

How will you know you are in the place inside that knows? Steer with your intention. Intention is the force that moves you. Just as you can direct yourself to stand or walk or sit, so too can you direct yourself to right action. Intuition is like an inner prayer. Listen and trust.

In her book *The Dynamic Laws of Prosperity*, Catherine Ponder talks about the "yes" and "no" phases of intuition:

> "There are **'yes'** and **'no'** phases of intuition. Often the **'yes'** phase of intuition comes in such a quiet, gentle way that you are inclined to disregard its promptings, at least at first. It does not try to convince you of anything. Usually, though, if you disregard it, the same hunch will gently tap at your mind again and again, until you do become aware of it.
>
> The **'no'** phase of intuition is often more pronounced. For years, it seemed that the only time my intuition ever came alive was

14

when it would emphatically say **'no'** to me through an inner feeling of restlessness, discomfort, or discontent. The **'no'** phase of intuition often seems louder and more emphatic. It gives you an uncomfortable feeling that you cannot cast off unless you follow your **'no'** guidance."

Intuition can keep you safe from danger. It can bring you peace in times of change. Intuition can bring you into your own authenticity and lead you forward to the truest, best, most real you.

Intuition will not make every decision fast or easy. It will make some choices easier. Sometimes experiences need to churn for a while. But when you know your intuition is speaking to you, LISTEN. When you feel your intuition tugging at you, PAY ATTENTION.

"As soon as you trust yourself,
you will know how to live."
– Goethe

Defining Boundaries

"Your freedom to swing your arms about
ends where my nose begins."

–Oliver Wendell Holmes

Creating personal boundaries for yourself and others is not as easy or as clear as marking the physical boundaries of a plot of land in real estate. But you need to set some.

How do you know where to set your personal boundaries? Go inside your own heart, mind, or guts to discern what is okay and what is not okay for you. It's a getting-in-touch-with-yourself exercise that takes effort and participation and awareness. If you let yourself "go to sleep" in this area, you risk much.

When I was a teenager in the seventies, I remember talking with a couple of friends. We laughed about people who would do anything for money. We made up a game show called "What's Your Price?" People would bid for gross things to do for money. We laughed at the idea. "How much money would it take for you to . . . (fill in the blank—like eat something gross or do something disgusting)?" I can't tell you how disappointed I am to see real shows on television today in which young people compromise themselves to do things for money that, under normal circumstances, would be unthinkable. What I considered a joke thirty years ago is what some people today compromise their dignity for.

Do you have boundaries in place that can never be moved? Once when telling my kids just how much I treasure them, I said that if someone offered me a million dollars, I would not trade them away. Amazed at that, they tried to raise the "price." Their faces lit up when they realized that no amount of money or gold or riches of any kind could ever tempt me to let them go. All children take great comfort in the embrace of a tight boundary that shows how much they are valued.

Appropriate boundaries help us create our world: they keep us safe when we keep them firm, and they help us grow as we let them loose.

If someone does or says something that violates your boundaries, it's up to you to call it. I'm not talking about extreme cases when you can't control the situation—that is another matter.

When you let people know you're a live wire, they won't step on you! What does this mean? If you saw an exposed electrical wire and knew it would shock you if you stepped on it, you wouldn't step on it, right? When you are aware of what is not acceptable—what you will not allow to be done to you or around you—you can set the right boundaries. You are in charge. (Just like the electrical "charge" of a live wire.) Setting boundaries means being able to say or do something to stop an intrusion you don't like. It might be mild and gentle or strong and assertive, depending on who you are talking with and the situation at hand.

Boundaries are around your body,
your speech, your emotions, your finances.
You have to set your own limits.
And until you get clear about
your own boundaries,
people will test you.

When someone asks you to do something and you say yes when you wanted to say no, you have allowed your boundaries to get fuzzy. You didn't set it up for yourself. This could be something simple like a time-consuming favor someone asks you to do. What if someone teases you, "What's wrong with a hug?!" when you really don't want to touch that person? Do you push your boundaries out to make someone else "feel" okay? Once you allow people to intrude on your boundaries, even out of misguided kindness, you may be setting yourself up for being taken advantage of, for compromising your integrity, or even for putting yourself in real danger.

JUST SAY "NO" WHEN YOU NEED TO SAY "NO"

It is okay to say "no!" Really. Kind people say "no." Other people say "no." It is mature to say "no" when that's what you mean. "No, thank you." "Really, no." "No." "Is there a reason you're not honoring my 'no'?"

I don't know who originally said this: *The best way to get what you want is to say 'no' to what you don't want.*

- No, I can't talk on the phone now.

- No to sex when it is not what you really want.

- No, I won't tease or bully to be "in" with a group.

- No to that business "opportunity!"

- No to people who are abusive.

- No to gossip.

- No to whatever does not serve you or what you want to create in your life.

The author of *The Gift of Fear*, Gavin DeBecker, teaches that when you say "no" and the person you say it to does not honor it, they are trying to control you. Pay attention when that happens and remember that the best way to get what you want is to say "no" to what you don't want.

That is powerful.

MILGRAM'S EXPERIMENT

In the early 1960s, an experimental psychologist named Stanley Milgram was motivated to know how so many people were able to murder MILLIONS in the Holocaust (can you even fathom that millions of people were murdered in such a violent, mechanical way?) and in the end simply say, "I was just following orders." So he conducted a study on conformity and obedience to authority.

There were three people involved:

1) the experimenter

2) the confederate (looked like a volunteer but was really in on the study)

3) the volunteer participant whose behavior was
   being studied
   (this person answered an ad to participate).

The participant would arrive at around the same time as the confederate and they would both be briefed on a study about "memory." The volunteer was told that s/he would be the "teacher" and the other would be the "student." The "teacher" (the volunteer) was directed to teach the "student" (the confederate) a series of word pairs. The teacher would watch the student being hooked up to electrodes and restrained. Then, from an adjacent room, the "teacher" would say something (related to word pairs) and the "student" would have to give the answer. If the answer was not correct, the "teacher" was to give an electrical shock of increasing intensity.

As far as the volunteer "teacher" knew, the shocks were real, although in fact they were not. Each incorrect answer and subsequent "shock" had a reaction that the "teacher" could hear. The reactions began as startled or "ouch" and increased to dramatic cries of pain. Each time the volunteer increased the intensity of the shock. The dial had labels on a scale leading up to "DANGER: SEVERE SHOCK" followed by "XXX." Whenever the volunteers to the study began to hesitate or question if they should continue, they were told by the "authority" to continue, even when they were terribly uncomfortable with the whole thing. THEY DID. The majority of the volunteers continued to shock the "student" until a final scream came and there was silence. Even when they doubted if they should continue, they did— ALL BECAUSE THE AUTHORITY TOLD THEM TO!

The tricky thing to face when exploring the lessons from this study is that these were regular folks, just like you and me. Homemakers, students, business folk. It was a frightening realization that these people could be pushed that way. It is easy for us to rationalize: "Well, it's a university campus, they wouldn't do anything dangerous." But the study wasn't always done in that format. Sometimes it was done so that the subject had no idea who was running the experiment. It is also easy for us to sit in the comfort of our world and exclaim, "I wouldn't have done it." That's what we can say AFTER we know the whole story.

HOW DOES THIS TRANSLATE?
How do we apply the lessons from this study?

- Wake up to yourself—know who you are, what you stand for, what is important to you.

- Wake up to what your gut tells you—consistently plug into your own inner voice and trust what you hear.

- Know your values, set your boundaries, and be firm when necessary. Now you know. Now you know that in any situation you have the power to choose. You choose your boundaries. You choose when and how to keep them. You receive the benefits and consequences (both positive and negative) of the boundaries you hold.

An encouraging part of Milgram's discovery was about the people involved in the study who *did* refuse the orders of the experimenter:

"I started with the belief that every person who came to the laboratory was free to accept or to reject the dictates of authority. This view sustains a conception of human dignity insofar as it sees in each man a capacity for choosing his own behavior. And as it turned out, many subjects did, indeed, choose to reject the experimenter's commands, providing a powerful affirmation of human ideals."

–From Milgram's reply to Baumrind's ethical critique of the obedience experiments, 1964

THE TRICKY THING ABOUT BOUNDARIES

You may hold certain values that will create a firm boundary in some areas. The tricky thing about boundaries is that the limits you set may need to change depending on what the situation is, who is involved, and where you are in your life. A couple of simple examples:

Your space is your space. People may not enter your home without knocking, but if you have friends who are very familiar, they may walk in unannounced, without knocking, and it's okay. Your boundaries change according to the people involved. Or if you have a house guest, you may even give them a key to your home to come and go. You have *temporarily* moved your boundary.

For religious Jews, driving on the Sabbath is forbidden. It's a very strong boundary for those who observe it. Yet, to save a life, the laws of Sabbath must be broken. A boundary that is totally firm in one situation disappears under other circumstances.

A child is taught not to speak with strangers because they have not developed their judgment. Adults speak with strangers all the time. Sharing a smile with someone you haven't met—a stranger—can lift your day and the day of the person who receives it.

So you need to judge each situation for what it is, keeping in mind the whole picture of who you are, what you want, what you are trying to accomplish. What is your message to yourself and others?

It's your world and your choice.
Build your boundaries with purpose and intention.

DON'T PANIC

"I'm not afraid of storms,
for I'm learning how to sail my ship."

–Louisa May Alcott

During a class to become a lifeguard, the instructor was grilling us on the steps to take if someone is in trouble in the water. He began with a question: What is the first thing you do when you see someone drowning? We each had our answer: "jump in" or "throw a line." He took us by surprise when he said, "Don't panic." After we absorbed that, he gave us the second part of the lifeguard strategy: EVALUATE THE SITUATION.

Staying calm and then assessing what needs to be done will save a lot of time and energy in the long run. In a life-and-death situation, the best choice of action may save just a few moments, but even a minute can make the difference between life and death!

Don't panic, and evaluate the situation. This is a really brilliant way to walk through life, which has a way of surprising us with the unexpected. There is no escaping the unforeseen surprises. But we have to face what we have to face. There is a philosophy that says we are never given more than we can handle. That means that in any given situation, you have the capacity to deal with it. It may not be fun or comfortable, but people have survived very dramatic, traumatic events in life. Some people have even faced evil in the extreme in this world. Somehow, within each one of them, a place inside has seen them through. Sometimes even great joy can be intense to process. It is wise to operate from a place inside our own minds and bodies and emotions that is centered as much as possible.

CENTERED DECISION MAKING
What does it mean to be centered? Imagine it with your body. If you have ever studied martial arts, for example, they teach you that there are ways to stand so that your center of gravity is low and you cannot be easily knocked

Key Steps for Decision Making

1. Don't panic—keep your balance.
2. Evaluate the situation—get perspective, see clearly what is happening.
3. Take action.

down. If you are standing as strong as you can muster, but not keeping the center of gravity low, you literally become a pushover. Staying emotionally centered means that you are the one in control of your emotional responses, not the person next to you. That's not to say that what others say or do doesn't have an impact, but you get to consciously choose the direction of your response.

Panic or anger, fear or defensiveness—or whatever your automatic reaction might be—cuts you off from the source within you that can guide you. Knowing where your center is gives you back your personal power. Even when you catch yourself "reacting," if you know where you want to be, you can get yourself there. Plug into your intuition, common sense, or whatever knowledge and resources you have within you. It's okay to seek counsel. Make sure you ask someone who you know will support you in making the choices that put you on the high road.

We journey through this life and life journeys through us. The gifts of life, time, and free will are ours. Although there may be a lot that we cannot control or choose, the perspective we hold and the actions we take are the tools to shape who we are and what we want to become. Finding your balance in the way you see and do things is a way of bringing harmony into your life.

There are some basic questions you can ask yourself in any given situation that arises in your world.

- What is my perspective? Does this perspective serve me? Do I need to shift the way I look at things? What really matters to me?

- Are my actions lining up to create the life I want? What is my next step?

- Am I in balance? Am I in a good position to make a decision? Are my thoughts clear, do I feel emotionally steady?

Keep in mind that your *perspective* (the way you think, see, feel about any given issue) and your *action* (what you do or do not do and even the intention you put into that action) are the foundation for building the life you want. Remember that you can always choose to change either your perspective or the direction of your actions if you want to adjust the way things are going in your life. Learning how to find and keep your center of *balance*, and how to operate and make decisions from that place, will keep you more effectively on the course you set for yourself.

BALANCE

"Perhaps too much of everything is as bad as too little."
–Edna Ferber

Balance is a way of measuring one thing against another, a means of decision making or judging, and it is also a steadiness in your mind, body, and emotions. The tricky thing about balance is that everyone has a different center of balance. The only way to access that center is from the inside and since no one else can get inside you, you have to find this one on your own. People who are close to you can have an influence by supporting you in finding that center, asking the right questions and so forth. Spending time with people who impose their ideas on you can cause you to lose touch with the place inside where you have your best balance.

The other tricky thing is that your center will change as you grow in knowledge and life experience. Did you ever watch a puppy from a large breed growing? It is good for some smiles. They seem to grow so fast, their feet get bigger and they have to completely adjust to their new bodies (like going up stairs) with each growth spurt. Our bodies also, as they mature (from infancy through adolescence, young adulthood into middle age and old age), will need adjustments in the way we treat them. So too, our minds, emotions, and the actions we take will need to be kept in balance from within.

What is good for one person is dangerous to another. When one person gives five dollars to charity, it is stingy; for another, it may be quite generous. Doing something kind for someone may be the biggest gift you can give yourself. Saying "no," on the other hand, may be the thing that keeps you sane. Everyone has a different balance. The only one who knows what you need to keep your own balance is you. In gymnastics, if you are walking on the balance beam, your coach can tell you to look straight ahead, put your arms out, feel the balance point in your body. But you are the one on the balance beam, you are the one who will fall if you lose your balance. *You* are the one who gets back up again. And it is you who will taste the sweetness of your success.

PERSPECTIVE

"What we see depends mainly on what we look for."
–John Lubbock

Perspective is one of the major factors in being the kind of person you want to be and creating the life you live. Example: There was a questionnaire going around on the internet which included the question, "Is the glass half full or half empty?" I sent it out and two different people answered it by saying, "It is overflowing." On one hand, you can look at the same glass and see it two different ways. On the other hand, you can ignore the first two choices and enjoy the one you create for yourself.

Other people and situations can influence or manipulate your perspective, but there can come a time in your life when you "wake up" to the notion that you are the one who is ultimately in control. Through your free will, you can hold, adopt and see the perspective you want.

Illustration ©Roger N. Shepard, 1990

There is more than one image in this picture. How many do you see? Just because you don't see the other picture right away doesn't mean it's not there, it just means you don't get it yet. Sometimes when we look at a picture, we don't see it until someone points it out. Once we are aware of its existence, we can see it any time we want. It's a great comfort that there is much yet to be revealed, that what we see isn't always all there is to see in any given situation.

In the picture above, you can see a man playing saxophone (in the black) or a woman's face (in the white).

What is an important accomplishment for a five-year-old is not a big deal at seventeen. We have to put things into context. On the other hand, something that has been mastered by a five-year-old—walking, for example—could be a major life accomplishment for an adult who has been through an accident and is relearning from the beginning.

"We don't see things as they are, we see them as we are."
–Anais Nin

ACTION

"I have seen soldiers panic at the first sight of battle,
and a wounded squire pulling arrows out from his
wound to fight and save his dying horse.
Nobility is not a birthright, but is defined by one's action."
–Kevin Costner, *Robin Hood, Prince of Thieves*

A theme that you'll find as a major turning point to creating your life and defining who you are and what you are about is the action you take or do not take. The extra good deed you do or do not do. The time you spend or do not spend with a loved one. What you put or do not put into your mouth. What you say or do not say. Remember that taking no action is a separate choice with its own consequences.

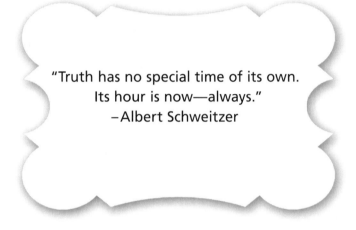

"Truth has no special time of its own.
Its hour is now—always."
–Albert Schweitzer

THE ONE PERCENT ADJUSTMENT

*It's never too late to have a life
and it's never too late to change one.*

When a rocket is sent into space, it is flying off its course more than it is on course! But it somehow reaches its destination. How? Course correction. It needs small but constant adjusting to keep it traveling on course to arrive where it's going. The "one percent adjustment" is making an easy change in your life—a course correction—which, over time, will have a huge payoff in results. Imagine two parallel lines going off into infinity: you know that they will never change. They will stay the same, never crossing, never venturing off into space. But adjust one of the lines (life choices—attitudes or actions) by even just one percent, and over distance (time) the change will be dramatic.

Imagine the lines continuing out. . . . Over time a simple adjustment will make a huge difference.

HOW THAT WORKS PRACTICALLY SPEAKING

When an athlete goes to compete, it is after many hours of practice. No athlete makes it to the top without coaching. The subtle adjustments made in the way they hold their body, the way they visualize the outcome, and their attitude, can make a huge impact on their performance. Having studied martial arts to an advanced belt, I learned that no matter how complicated things get, it always comes back to the basics. It is always about refining what you know and doing it the best you can, improving just a little bit each time. The results of improvement are instant, and over time each little improvement adds up.

In a way, each chapter in this book represents one of the many facets of life. Decide in which areas you want to make changes, read the ideas and experiment to see if the changes you make give you the improvement or advancement you want for yourself.

Whatever you choose, you'll increase your success by only trying something that is really doable for you. That means not biting off more than you can chew comfortably. It means taking small baby steps so you can enjoy the journey and the success along the way.

Make adjustments that are simple. But do make a commitment. And know that the commitment you make is really to yourself. Learn one more new thing, just one at a time. A small shift will have dramatic impact.

There is a story about a woman whose house was a mess. Nothing seemed to be in place anywhere, a real disaster. One day an elderly neighbor gave her a red geranium plant for a gift.

As the young woman put the plant on the kitchen table, she thought it would be a good idea to just clear off the table from the stuff that was piled up so she could really enjoy the beauty of the flowering plant. Once the table was all cleaned off she stood back to admire the plant and the way the sun came in the room. She noticed how the cluttered, messy counters of her kitchen looked in contrast to the clear table, so she just straightened out the kitchen counters. The room looked great and she sat down to enjoy a cup of tea.

When she walked from the kitchen to the living room, she noticed the contrast once again between the neat kitchen and the messy room.So she decided to clean that room as well. Moving from one room to the next, the entire house was finally clean.

What is your "red geranium?" What simple adjustment can you make?

WHAT DO YOU EXPECT?

"Blessed are those that naught expect,
for they shall not be disappointed."

–John Wolcott

Here is one of those keys that will help you in your relationships, including the one with yourself. As with all of our options for attitude, we can also control our interpersonal expectations—that is, what we expect of others and what we lead them to expect of us. When you set your expectations at a reasonable level, you allow yourself to be pleased more often than disappointed. When you help others set their expectations of you, you can contribute to creating positive relations.

When a contractor is building a house, there are many factors out of his control for which he must take responsibility. He doesn't know when other people who are doing the work are going to be sick or late. He can't control the weather for rain or snow. So, if he's smart, he does his best to set a date that will be realistic for completion. On the other hand, the buyer/homeowner would be wise to consider that it is likely that the work will not be complete at exactly the time predicted.

Disappointment is a part of life, but it is always nice when you don't have to feel others' disappointment directed at you. If you expect that from time to time people will do things that disappoint you, when it shows up, you can keep your perspective and it will be much easier to handle.

When you are in a work situation, you are expected to perform the tasks at hand, in the way and timing that you agreed to when you accepted the job. It is also reasonable to ask the employer what you can expect in return: money, benefits, etc. When you don't meet the expectations of your boss, you get fired. When you exceed those expectations, you get a raise or promotion. I once heard a man telling someone about a carpenter. He said, "He's slow, but very detailed." This gives a realistic perspective, and gives choices like, do I want the work done cheaply or well?

When you go into a department store and are paying a lot of money for something, your expectation for the level of service is high. So if the sales clerk is nowhere to be found you are disappointed. When you have a high expectation but are not given much, it's a disappointing—maybe even aggravating—experience. On the other hand, when you have a low expectation but the level of service is high, you are pleased.

GET REAL
Get real about what you can expect from the people around you.

I expect my kids to have good manners. The smaller they are, the smaller my expectations and the more the training. When they don't meet my expectations, they will get feedback. When they exceed my expectations and are great with guests, I can fly high. But then, I have to adjust my expectations to who they are. At four or five years old, they can't sit like an adult.

In a marriage, I have certain expectations of my husband as he does of me. I do expect him to be faithful to me. I don't expect flowers every night. These are, of course, the obvious examples. Let's get a bit more subtle. I expect my husband to listen when I need to talk with him. I don't expect him to hang up on a business call when I want to talk. He expects me to wait for an appropriate opening.

It is helpful to discuss with people you are in relationship with what you can expect from them and what they can expect from you. If you are smart, you will especially do this before committing yourself to a marriage, a roommate, a job, a partner in any kind of project, a travel mate. Any time you plan to spend any amount of time with someone, talking about what you can realistically expect and what others can expect from you is smart.

- Expect changes.
- Expect disappointment.
- Expect to be amazed in life.
- Expect surprises.
- Expect the unexpected.

Things Aren't Always As They Seem

There is a story about a man who was given the chance to travel with the prophet Elijah. The offer was conditional: the man was not to ask questions about the ways of the prophet. The moment he did, he would lose his opportunity and be sent back home.

The first stop was the home of a poor couple. Their home was hardly more than a hut, but there they lived content with what they had. When the couple saw the two men at the door, they offered to share their small portion of food as they invited the visitors in. In the morning, the couple's main source of income, the cow from which they got milk, was dead. The two guests thanked their hosts and left. The man looked at the prophet in disbelief. How could he repay the couple's kindness with the death of their cow? He remained silent as they traveled on.

The next stop was the home of a wealthy man. When they came to the door, the servant of the house told them to go away, there was nothing for them there. The prophet pleaded with the servant asking for a corner on the floor so they would at least have shelter from the night and the cold. Finally the servant went to the master of the house, who agreed to let the two stay on a pile of straw in the unfinished basement of the estate. In the morning, the walls to the basement were finished.

At this point the man could no longer remain silent. As the two travelers left to continue on their way, the man turned to Elijah and cried out: "How could it be that the couple who was so kind and generous would be made to lose their cow, and the wealthy man who was so stingy with us would awaken to find the work in his home complete?!"

Elijah turned to the man and reminded him that their time together would come to an end if he answered the question. The man was willing to pay this price for an answer, and so Elijah gave it:

"Things are not always as they seem to be. The night we stayed at the home of the kind couple, the angel of death came for the wife. I had him take the cow instead so they could have more years together.

"As for the wealthy man who was so greedy and selfish," the prophet continued, "there was another fortune buried within the wall of his basement. Had the work been finished by laborers, the riches would have been discovered by the wealthy man."

Things are not always as they seem.

EXPECT MIRACLES

*"There are only two ways to live your life.
One is as though nothing is a miracle. The other is as
though everything is a miracle."*

– Albert Einstein

Miracles are a fact of life. Once you look for them, you will see them. A miracle like the splitting of the sea is not something that happens these days. But the miracle of birth happens every moment. It is no less a miracle just because it happens frequently.

Miracles can be explained away. That's one of the interesting things about them. Two people can look at the same event and see something completely different. You see what you look for. The attitude of seeing the wonder of life and all that surrounds you will nourish you and carry you through tough times. We all know that there are tough times; no one escapes pain in this world. Wouldn't it be amazing to be able to look at even the most painful experiences and see in them miracles and gifts? Often we don't see the gifts right away. That doesn't mean they are not there.

Have you ever been on the road in a big hurry when the driver in front of you seems to be going maddeningly slowly? You could have made that light up ahead if you could have just gotten by her. But as you pull up to the intersection, you can see the guy turning left has no regard for anything but getting through his turn. Had you been just a few feet ahead, he would've plowed right into you. Sometimes we don't see the near misses because we forget to consider the whole picture.

That's where trust comes in. Things don't always turn out the way you think they should. Consider adopting the attitude that every outcome is always to your advantage. You might not know it until some time later. Things aren't always what they seem.

When you look for miracles, they become daily occurrences. I needed help one day because I was particularly overwhelmed and dealing with a sinus infection. I called someone who was able to come that afternoon. When she got to my house, she told me that it was very unusual for her to have that space open and any other day she would have had to turn me down. I consider that a miracle and a gift.

Have you ever had something happen in the most coincidental timing? A comedian had in his routine a line he kept repeating: "Coincidence? I think not!" I love that line. Again, what kind of life do you want to have? Sometimes I can't help but ask my son, "What kind of day do you want to have?" I want him to know that he gets to choose his day by his attitude. We all do. *How might the attitude of looking for and expecting miracles change things for you?*

> "The invariable mark of wisdom
> is to see the miraculous in the common."
> –Ralph Waldo Emerson

You can look for the miraculous all around you, in each moment. Recognizing and acknowledging the miracles— whether through journaling, a whispered prayer, or whatever else you can think of—keeps the miracles coming. And keeps you aware of the gifts that are all around you. I remember going out with a friend one evening when her kids were small. They were watching TV when she kissed them good-bye. As we were walking out the door, the kids cried out, "But you didn't kiss us good-bye!" Of course, I had just seen her do it. The kids were so distracted by the TV that they didn't even notice the loving kiss from their mother. How often are we "kissed" but so distracted that we don't notice it?

> "Hope is the companion of power, and mother of success; for who so hopes strongly has within him the gift of miracles."
> –Samuel Smiles

IT'S YOUR CHOICE

Alice came to a fork in the road.
"Which road do I take?" she asked.
"Where do you want to go?"
responded the Cheshire cat.
"I don't know," Alice answered.
"Then," said the cat, "it doesn't matter."

–Lewis Carroll, *Alice in Wonderland*

In each and every moment you make choices. There are choices about the actions you take to direct your life. Simple choices: if you eat this, then you do not eat that. If you wear this, you do not wear that. Or bigger choices: you'll live here, not there. You'll marry this person, and close the door to others. There are choices you make to direct your character: whether or not you stop to help someone in need, the tone of voice and the words you use to communicate with the people around you. There are choices you make in directing your attitude. Are you giving the benefit of the doubt where appropriate in relationships? Are you expressing gratitude? Are you awake to the possibility and potential of each day?

Where you sit now is a culmination of the choices you have made up until this point. The older you get, the less you can blame circumstance. Take responsibility. Because you always have the power to choose. Ultimately, it comes down to each one of us understanding that we are responsible for the choices we make, that the power of choice is always in our hands within any set of circumstances. This is our privilege as human beings, our free will.

You are the only one who ultimately makes the decisions for yourself. "Do I have to?" is the cry of many children. Authorities may tell them that they "have to" do something, yet there really is a choice. A child may not like the consequences of a choice they make. You may not like the consequences of the choices you make. You don't have to be to school or work on time. But being late may mean losing something that is important. You don't even have to go to school at all. For some people the choice to drop out of school has disastrous results. For others, it means the independence to build what they know they were meant to build in the first place and is their road to success.

CONTROL AND CHOICE

The variety of choices we have changes depending on many factors. A child does not have so much control over his environment, his family, etc. The country you live in plays a part in the range of choices that you have. You may be able to influence your health, money, and strength, but these domains also have limits that can define your options. Obviously there are many things that are just simply out of our hands. At the same time, no matter what, you still have free choice or free will. Though a person's body may be in chains, their spirit still has free will.

During the Holocaust of World War II, millions of people were murdered in sadistic, systematic ways by Adolph Hitler and his Nazi party in Germany. The horror spread throughout Europe as Hitler attempted to exterminate a whole race of people, the Jews. Hitler and his Nazis murdered many others in their path: cripples, gays, gypsies, and political dissidents. All of this within the last century, not even ancient history.

Hitler built horrific death camps and labor camps. These were places where mass murder took place, as well as grotesque tortures of the human body and psyche. There were some survivors, most of whom were very young at the time, and many of whom have now passed on. Viktor Frankl was one of those who survived the Holocaust and the camps. He wrote a book called *Man's Search for Meaning*. In this book, he tells the unfathomable story of his experiences in the camps. If ever there was a situation where a person seemed to have no choices, this was it. Yet Frankl writes that the opposite was true: even in the midst of hell, man can always choose how to act:

"I may give the impression that the human being is completely and unavoidably influenced by his surroundings. (In this case the surroundings being the unique structure of camp life, which forced the prisoner to conform his conduct to a certain set pattern.) But what about human liberty? Is there no spiritual freedom in regard to behavior and reaction to any given surroundings? Is that theory true which would have us believe that man is no more than a product of many conditional and environmental factors —be they of a biological, psychological, or sociological nature? Does man have no choice of action in the face of such circumstances?

We can answer these questions from experience as well as on principle. The experiences of camp life show that man does have a choice of action. There were enough examples, often of a heroic nature, which proved that apathy could be overcome, irritability suppressed. Man can reserve a vestige of spiritual freedom, of independence of mind, even in such terrible conditions of psychic and physical stress.

We who lived in concentration camps can remember the men who walked through the huts comforting others, giving away their last piece of bread. They may have been few in number, but they offer sufficient proof that everything can be taken from a man but one thing: the last of the human freedoms—to choose one's own way.

And there were always choices to make. Every day, every hour, offered the opportunity to make a decision, a decision which determined whether you would or would not submit to those powers which threatened to rob you of your very self, your inner freedom; which determined whether or not you would become the plaything of circumstance, renouncing freedom and dignity to become molded into the form of the typical inmate. . . .

Fundamentally, therefore, any man can, even under such circumstances, decide what shall become of him—mentally and spiritually. He may retain his human dignity even in a concentration camp. . . .

It is this spiritual freedom—which cannot be taken away—that makes life meaningful and purposeful."

The choices you make get you where you want to be and allow you to become who you want to be. Every choice you make has a consequence. Sometimes you like the results of your choices, sometimes not. Even when you pick something that did not have the results you wanted or expected, you have the opportunity to grow and move forward. It can be awesome, scary, and liberating all at the same time to know that you have the power to move and create for yourself in this world.

Attitudes, goals, friends, jobs, emotions, image, values, posture. The choice is yours.

"There will be winters in your life.
Some people freeze to death, some people ski!"
–Tony Robbins

Accountability

"The people who get on in this world are the people who get up and look for the circumstances they want, and, if they can't find them, make them."

–George Bernard Shaw

One of the reasons I wanted to write this book in the first place was to maybe save someone the possibility of some heartache. If you pay attention to this short chapter and can "get it," the rewards could be reflected for years to come. On the other hand, there are things you can do that you'll pay for, maybe even for the rest of your life. It doesn't work to blame others. Circumstances are not always in your control, but the choices you make are all yours. That's accountability.

ONE THOUGHTLESS CHOICE TODAY
CAN CHANGE YOUR LIFE FOREVER

"Boys will be boys" is an excuse often given when a boy, or even young man, behaves impulsively. A wide range of behaviors is excused, waved away with this throwaway line.

Sometimes when parents or teachers don't want to get involved and intervene with teens, they change the line to "teens will be teens." If you haven't gotten training in responsible behavior, you need to learn right here and now that what you do can and will impact the whole rest of your life.

*Jimmy** (starred names are changed) was a teenager, eighteen to be exact. He was goofing around one day and made a choice that will follow him the rest of his adult life. He committed a crime. It wasn't really a big deal, he was really just a wild guy. But Jimmy wound up in jail. For sure it was not fun and although he was released rather quickly, he now has a record that says he was arrested for a felony.

The sad thing is that Jimmy is a great guy. It's only a couple of years since his jail time but he's grown a lot in that short time. He's trustworthy and nice, loyal, a good man. After the tragedy at the World Trade Center, Jimmy wanted to enlist into the army service. But guess what? They wouldn't take him!

*Maurice** was twenty, his girlfriend was seventeen—underage. They were crazy about each other at the time. They were sexually active. No big deal in these times, right? To his girlfriend's father, it was a big deal. He had Maurice prosecuted. He spent three months in jail. With that felony, he has also lost privileges in society that others take for granted. For his whole adult life. With the distinct possibility that he could live to be eighty years of age or more, that means he pays a price for sixty years for something he did at twenty!

*Annie** is an attractive, sweet, smart young woman. She fell in love with a charming, handsome young man and they spent a lot of time together. When he told her he needed a short-term loan of some money—it was a rather large sum for someone so young—Annie lent him the money her grandfather had left her. The money is gone for good and you don't need to be a genius to guess that the guy is, too.

*Lindsay** knew at fourteen that she wanted a baby. Every adult in her life tried to convince her that would not be wise. At seventeen she had the baby that she so much wanted. She loves and adores her baby, and when the baby isn't with her grandmother, Lindsay can even be a pretty good mom. But as Lindsay has matured, she realized her choice to conceive was unwise. If she could turn the clock back and make the choice again, she would wait. She would wait for a healthier man to be in her life and the life of her child. She sacrificed the opportunities of her youth, something that can never be replaced.

If you do a thing out of ignorance, you are still accountable and you still have to pay the consequences. *Jean** was driving along in the parking lot, fiddling with the radio. She only looked down for a minute and it was just in that minute that she hit the other car. Sometimes you just don't get the power of a moving vehicle until you feel it crash into something. When *Carly** was fourteen she decided to take a joy ride on a busy street. Her crash, thankfully, had no injuries. *Jesse** and *Pat** were not so lucky. Sadly, they both died.

If you are smart, you can learn from your mistakes before there is permanent damage. Carly used her joy ride as a point of reference and got the huge learning of choices and consequences. Everyone makes mistakes and choices they regret. When you learn from your mistakes (or

OPM—Other People's Mistakes), you reset the direction you want to take and go from there.

The examples above are all real. They are all on the dramatic side. The thing is, there is no way around it: *If you are going to have a life, you are going to make mistakes.* The purpose of this conversation is that if you understand that there is a spectrum and you can learn the same lesson in a milder form or from someone else's experience, why not give yourself the gift of being awake while you make choices.

Take Responsibility

responsibility = response-ability:
your ability to respond to each life situation

Use your head. I imagine that in some of the examples above, you "saw it coming," you knew where I was going with the story. The people whose stories I share are just like the rest of us. They are all bright, attractive people, who didn't bother to take the time to think things through and understand what was at stake with their choices.

Use your guts. Listen to your inner voice. You have to get quiet with yourself for a bit to plug into your intuition. It's harder when you have friends pulling at you. Keep in mind that the friends who might mislead you will not be able to repair any damage that you have to live with. It's your life.

Pay attention to who you spend your time with. If you spend time with people who smoke, you are more likely to smoke. If you spend time with people who are financially successful, you are more likely to be financially successful. When I took driver's education in high school, they taught me that the direction you focus your eyes in is the direction your car will move. If you are watching the side of the road, your car will begin to move in that direction. *Where your attention goes, that's where you go.*

Take some time to make your choices. Some decisions require you to talk things over with someone, to really reflect. Some decisions need to be made in a moment. But a moment can be enough if you really take it and use it to check in with yourself, your head, heart, intuition. It's even okay to tell others that you need time to consider your choice if others are involved. Some choices have to be made in a flash. Those are usually life and death issues, on the road, etc. (I highly recommend you take a first aid class. It will give you training in the way to think when you have to make a quick decision.)

"Reacting" is done without consideration. You bang your head and react by saying "OW!" You take responsibility by closing the cabinet door you hit your head on.

In the movie *Fried Green Tomatoes,* Kathy Bates's character finds herself bullied by a couple of loudmouthed, rude teens. When she has her first encounter with them, she retreats. In her second, more confident encounter, she slams her car into theirs. As the audience, we laugh and cheer: her reaction takes us by surprise because we know that the consequences will carry a high cost. Maybe we fantasize about being able to do the same thing in the heat of the moment. There really are people who react in dangerous or foolish ways. Most of us know it will cost us time and money so we control the childish impulses.

Let's take it to a deeper level. In every moment, we have choices to make. Each choice results in a consequence, positive or negative. Taking responsibility means you pay attention to the feedback you get as you make your choices. Taking responsibility means you don't blame someone else for any given situation you are in. Taking responsibility means you ask yourself what you can do to change course if you are not moving in the direction that will really create the life you want to live.

Taking responsibility is not blaming others and staying stuck.

Responsibility is being awake to making the choices, using your own free will, doing what you can within any given situation, being your best over and over again. *When you are wondering if you are taking responsibility in a situation, one of the cues that you are NOT is that you are blaming someone or something else. (This is dangerous behavior and can lead to self pity and staying stuck in a bad place.)*

BALANCE YOUR BOOKS

In business, all your account books have to be balanced and clear. You have to know how much money you have earned, and how much you have paid out. When you do this accounting you can see if you are on track with your plan, moving in the direction of growth and profit. You can do a similar "accounting" of your life. Take a step back and take stock of your thoughts (perspective) and your deeds (actions). Take stock of your actions, because they create your life. Are you who you want to be? Are you making the choices to move in the direction of the life you want to live? If you need to make adjustments, what do you need to do? When will you do it? How will you do it? Do you need support?

"The great thing in this world is not so much where we stand, as in what direction we are moving."

−Oliver Wendell Holmes

Sam's Sandwiches

On a construction site in the Midwest, when the lunch whistle blew, all the workers would sit down together to eat. And with singular regularity Sam would open his lunch pail and start to complain.

"Son of a gun!" he'd cry, "not peanut butter and jelly sandwiches again. I hate peanut butter and jelly!"

Sam moaned about his peanut butter and jelly sandwiches day after day after day. Weeks passed, and the other workers were getting irritated by his behavior. Finally, another man on the work crew said, "Fer crissakes, Sam, if you hate peanut butter and jelly so much, why don't you just tell yer ol' lady to make you something different?"

"What do you mean, my ol' lady" Sam replied. "I'm not married. I make my own sandwiches."

–Dan Millman, *Way of the Peaceful Warrior*
(Novato, CA: New World Library, 2000)

An Autobiography in Five Short Chapters

I. I walk down the street. There is a deep hole in the sidewalk. I fall in. I am lost . . . I am helpless. It isn't my fault. It takes forever to find a way out.

II. I walk down the same street. There is a deep hole in the sidewalk. I pretend I don't see it. I fall in again. I can't believe I am in this same place. But it isn't my fault. It still takes a long time to get out.

III. I walk down the same street. There is a deep hole in the sidewalk. I see it is there. I still fall in—it's a habit. But, my eyes are open. I know where I am. It is my fault. I get out immediately.

IV. I walk down the same street. There is a deep hole in the sidewalk. I walk around it.

V. I walk down another street.

–Portia Nelson, *There's a Hole in My Sidewalk: The Romance of Self-Discovery*
(Hillsboro, OR: Beyond Words Publishing, 1993)

Part Two

Challenges

"I find the great thing in this world is not so much
where we stand, as in what direction we are
moving—we must sail sometimes with the wind and
sometimes against it—but we must sail,
and not drift or lie at anchor."

–Oliver Wendell Holmes, Jr.

FAILURE—MISSING THE MARK

"If you have made mistakes, even serious ones, there is always another chance for you. What we call failure, is not the falling down, but the staying down."

–Mary Pickford

When you experience failure with something—a test, a business deal, a sports competition, a relationship, whatever—the *way* you deal with it is the issue at hand, not the failure itself. *You* are not your experiences, but you do *have* your experiences to use as your ladder for growth.

When you feel like something you did was a failure it is so disappointing. But even with disappointment you can rise to redirect your thinking and perspective. You can take another approach to your goals and dreams. Move closer to what it is that you want.

Don't panic or put yourself down, neither of which will serve you. Evaluate the situation. Ask yourself these questions:

- What went wrong?

- What do I need to do, if anything, to correct the mistake?

- What did I learn from this?

- How would I do it differently today?

- Am I growing?

It is said that the definition of insanity is doing the same thing over and over, and expecting different results. It is kind of like dialing a wrong number on the telephone, hanging up and hitting the redial button to try again. When you get a wrong number, you check to make sure you are touching the correct keys or you look up the number in the phone book again, right?

If you are failing a class, maybe you need to drop the class and start over another time. Maybe you need a different teacher. Maybe you just didn't take the time to study. Maybe you need a tutor to understand some of the concepts.

Ask for feedback if you are not sure why you are failing. Any sport you play will be improved by coaching. Relationships sometimes need a little coaching.

Sometimes a failure just needs to be looked at in a different way. The glue used for sticky notes was invented by accident while the inventor was trying to create a whole different kind of glue.

Maybe a failed relationship will lead you to a better one. A failed job interview may give you the experience you need for an important interview later.

An important part in dealing with the disappointment of failure is to forgive yourself and others. It doesn't mean that you disregard behavior that is dangerous or hurtful. It does mean that you learn to let go where you need to.

Consider, "What's next?" Do you need more clarity? A different approach? To let go? Do you need to keep moving or take a break to renew yourself?

What happens when you fail? How can you deal with it? Take a deep breath and do the best you can from there. There is a spectrum of life experiences that we have before us. Some of the things we do have small consequences and some have a much higher price tag. MISTAKES ARE FEEDBACK TO YOU. Failure can tell you that you are on the wrong course: time to change directions. Sometimes failure is there to challenge you to rise. The challenge is that *you* are the one with your own best answers. Even when you hear an idea from someone else, or receive the feedback someone gives you on your way to evaluating your situation, it is you and you alone who draws up the courage to take the next step.

Failure is also a matter of perspective. FAILURE IS AN OPPORTUNITY TO GROW. Can failure actually be a step on the road to success? Yes.

This "Failure List" has many variations and can get pretty long. Here are a few examples:

- Einstein was four years old before he could speak.

- Isaac Newton did poorly in grade school and was considered "unpromising."

- Beethoven's music teacher once said of him, "As a composer he is hopeless."

- When Thomas Edison was a youngster, his teacher told him he was too stupid to learn anything. He was counseled to go into a field where he might succeed by virtue of his pleasant personality.

- F.W. Woolworth got a job in a dry goods store when he was twenty-one, but his employer would not permit him to wait on customers because he "didn't have enough sense to close a sale."

- Michael Jordan was cut from his high school basketball team. Boston Celtics Hall of Famer Bob Cousy suffered the same fate.

- A newspaper editor fired Walt Disney because he "lacked imagination and had no good ideas."

- Winston Churchill failed the sixth grade.

- Babe Ruth struck out thirteen hundred times— a major league record.

There are stories about many musicians including the Beatles, writers including Dr. Seuss, and business people including the Colonel (of KFC fame) who were rejected time and time again. What if they had not taken one more step in the direction of their dreams? What if the failure or rejection was the "kick in the rear" they may have needed at the time? You get the idea.

No one is great in everything across the board. You have to pick what is important to you, and work on that area for yourself. Sometimes we need to "step up to the plate" and be responsible, even if it wouldn't be our first choice in this moment.

What if you're fired from a job? So? Did you show up? Did you meet expectations? Were you responsible? Was it just time to grow or move on? Sometimes *you* know it's time to move on, but when *you* don't take the steps, things happen anyway. One famous personality kept getting fired and each time got a better job until she got her own show!

What if you fail a class? So? So you have to repeat it? Have a look at *why* you failed the class. Was it too advanced? Did you not stay current? Were you intimidated? Did you not care?

Did a relationship fall apart? You may need time to grieve. But the feeling of failure is temporary. Use the idea that there is something for you to learn about yourself in this experience. Find your balance, move on, and take what you need to grow and do better next time.

FAILURE IS A TIME TO REFLECT ON WHAT IS IMPORTANT. From there you can make choices about what is next. Reflection is an important part in the process of growth.

"I have learned that in order to increase the number of my successes, I have to accept an increase in the number of my failures. I think any success worth having is like a hundred-rung ladder. There's no use trying to jump in the middle; take it as a bottom-to-top proposition, one step at a time. Yes, to the faint of heart each of the 99 of those steps represents a failure of sorts. But to those with the determination to stay the course, success is inevitable."

–Harvey Mackay

HANDLING REGRET

"When one door of happiness closes, another opens;
but often, we look so long at the closed door
that we do not see the one
which has been opened for us."

–Helen Keller

I once heard that regret for things you did in the past fades with time, but regret for things left undone grows with time. I'm not sure that is entirely true; you can use a thought like this to rationalize doing something that you will regret later if you're not being entirely clear and honest with yourself. But I do see truth in it as well, because if you have a dream or desire to accomplish something or to travel or to take on some big project, and you ignore it, there may come a time when it is too late and you have missed the chance entirely.

Regret is a kind of feedback mechanism within us. Regret is an opportunity to review, renew, and re-approach our lives to return to the truth of who we are, what we are about, and who we truly want to be out in the world. Regret makes us face ourselves in the mirror, makes us face our souls. And, as with everything else, there is a necessary balance. Regret is a good thing in some ways; it lets us get to the truth of what is in our hearts. The trick is to have a look at what we regret doing (or not doing), make up our mind to change the way we do something in the future, and then do it.

Forgiving yourself is a big step to moving past the regret.

Redirecting your energy is important. What is redirecting? Think of a little trickle of water on a dirt road in the mountains. It can continue to deepen and widen and damage the road, unless you dig a gutter to redirect the flow.

What do you regret? Hurting someone might need an apology, perhaps a financial, material repair. You may be able to balance—or redirect—the regret you feel for a wrong you've done to someone by doing acts of kindness.

Is your regret for stupid choices you've made? You can redirect that regret by realizing that you have learned and would not make the same choice today.

Acknowledging mistakes is important, but spending time in self-pity about it is useless. Let the mistake be like the pulling back of a bow: although there is tension in the string, it is the very thing you can use to propel yourself forward. Direct your actions to do good; it is healing. Direct your thoughts to forgiveness; it also is healing.

"You are wallowing in useless remorse—
I'll have to ask you to stop."
–The Doctor, Star Trek Voyager

Notice where you feel the regret and use it as feedback. Change what you need to, correct your course, then let it go.

"Life is true, every step of it Godly. Only the emptiness is false. There are things we regret. Things we want to tear out of our memory, rip out of our hearts with remorse and agony. But in the end, the thing we reject never was. From its birth it was not a thing, but an absence—that God was not there. Once that void is washed away with tears, there remains only a crystal jewel rescued from the deep earth."
–Menachem Schneerson

Trusting the Hard Times

"Trouble creates a capacity to handle it. I don't say embrace trouble. That's as bad as treating it as an enemy. But I do say, meet it as a friend, for you'll see a lot of it and had better be on speaking terms with it."

–Oliver Wendell Holmes

So often we have an expectation that if you don't have everything just right, it's all wrong. Sometimes you just feel like you're getting hit on the head with every wham the universe can send your way. The truth is—and it takes effort to get into this mindset—everything in our life is here to serve us in becoming our best. Not most perfect, just the best we can become. We may not have control over whether we can avoid suffering, but we are always in a position to make use of our fortune and misfortune to develop and reveal the best within us.

I was once in one of life's "trials" and it was pretty scary for me. I had already come to understand that everything happens to us for a reason. But this trial was so challenging and time consuming. I was emotionally spent. It happened that my path crossed with a woman who runs a clinic in pain management. Though my pain was not physical, she had just the right words of encouragement. But then she gave me more. As we talked about the situation, I looked at her and asked, "So why is all this happening?" She looked at me like I had asked her what is 2 + 2 and responded simply, "So you can grow!"

Growing is not a comfortable thing. That's why we hear about "growing pains." Getting familiar with the discomfort of growth can help you move through it more smoothly. All this does not mean that you sit passively as hard times hit. You need to participate: make the choices that are right for you, shift the way you look at things, and move on when it's time.

Attitude is the answer.

Attitude is the choice.

You get to choose how you look at each day and relationship, situation, issue. You get to choose your own perspective in every moment.

A PARABLE

A bunch of frogs were playing one bright day when the jumpiest of them fell into a deep hole. "Help, help!" he cried as he jumped and jumped to reach the top. His friends gathered around and called to him to jump higher. But the frog was so deep he couldn't hear his friends. They panicked about how they might help.

Along came the king frog who heard the ruckus and thought of an idea. They could push some rocks into the hole and the stuck frog could use them to climb out. Well, when the stones started flying into the hole and hitting the little green guy, he started to cry. He couldn't imagine why life would deal him such a harsh blow.

Then he got mad. He started to throw the rocks back. That was no help.The very rocks he threw at them never reached the top and rained right back down striking him again. It wasn't long until the floor of the hole was getting crowded and he was getting squished and smashed. He pulled himself up and climbed upon the pile of rocks. Looking up with tears in his eyes, he noticed that he was a bit closer to the top of the hole.

The rocks kept coming and that frog kept dodging and jumping up on top of them. The very thing he thought was sent to hurt him, was what he used to help himself. At last the frog jumped out of the hole and thanked the king for his kindness.

"Life's challenges are isometrics for the soul.
They force out its inner powers.
In every hardship, look for the spark of good and focus upon it with all your might. If you cannot find that spark, rejoice that wonder beyond your comprehension has befallen you."

–Menachem Schneerson

Good, Bad, Who Knows?

An old man and his son worked a small farm with only one horse to pull the plow. One day, the horse ran away.

"How terrible," sympathized the neighbors. "What bad luck."

"Who knows whether it is bad luck or good luck," the farmer replied.

A week later, the horse returned from the mountains, leading five wild mares into the barn.

"What wonderful luck!" said the neighbors.

"Good luck? Bad luck? Who knows?" answered the old man.

The next day the son, trying to tame one of the horses, fell and broke his leg.

"How terrible. What bad luck!"

"Bad luck? Good luck?"

The army came to all the farms to take the young men for war. The farmer's son was of no use to them, so he was spared.

"Good? Bad?"

–Dan Millman, *Way of the Peaceful Warrior*
(Novato, CA: New World Library, 2000)

Pain and Suffering

"Children are born with certain inalienable rights,
among them the right to fail, to hurt,
to suffer disappointment, to get angry, and mess up.
Without these traits, how would they know the triumph
of dealing with an illness, the pride of conquering
adversity, the exhilaration of turning their lives around,
the privilege of saying, 'I'm sorry.'"

–Erma Bombeck

Pain and suffering are a part of this world and this life. Where you live, the stage of life you are in, how you take care of yourself, and the attitude you hold, are all factors in the kind of pain and suffering you encounter and the way you perceive it and process it. What you need to know about pain and suffering is this:

No one can avoid pain and suffering.

One of the challenges of many young people today who are blessed enough to live in a world of plenty (and there are worlds of lack, starvation, and brutality within the many realities on this beautiful blue planet), is that loving parents have protected them from the reality of pain so that when the inescapable happens, they don't have a clue about how to be with it. For others, it may seem that pain and suffering are the theme of their lives. They need to wake up to their own personal power to connect, make changes, and heal.

Wherever you are on the spectrum, pain and suffering are a natural part of being human. It is not the part we run to or look forward to, but it is real for everyone. As you process your own or sit with someone else through their pain, know that although it does not feel like it during the heat of the pain:

It WILL pass.

The pain will not last forever. It may not pass as soon as you would like, but it will pass. King Solomon was known for his great wisdom. There are many stories about the righteous judgments he gave in difficult cases. It is told of King Solomon that he wore a ring on his finger that he could look at whenever he was feeling great pain. It said, "This too shall pass." Then, when he was celebrating great joy, he could turn the ring and it said, "This too shall pass." Nothing is permanent. Like the weather (which is no small thing in itself—a reflection of the mystery of creation), life has cycles.

Pain and suffering are necessary to grow.

I am not suggesting that you seek pain; on the contrary, do what you can to stay in joy for yourself and those around you. At the same time, understand that suffering has its rewards, and they are rich if you step into the strength to reap the lessons. Find the place inside you that has the strength to support and love the place inside you that feels the pain.

For people who have not ever let themselves fully face their pain, it might seem like if you let yourself go with it, it might just consume you and you'll be out of control and lose yourself. The thing is, there is always another side to experiencing pain: healing. Your suffering gives you empathy to the pain and suffering of others. Empathy, the ability to understand another's pain, allows you to connect. Connecting is healing. When you are present for someone else in pain, in helping them heal, you help yourself heal, too.

Where you are is not where you will wind up.

Sometimes life puts us "on trial." We are tested, molded, sharpened, polished. While we are in the hard times of life— the challenges—we are being given an experience that will shape us for THE BETTER in the long run.

Sometimes being in a dark, down, lonely, ineffective, helpless place feels like it is eternity and will never be any different.

In Colorado there is an expression: "If you don't like the weather, just wait a bit and it will change." It's like that in all of life. If you don't like the situation, have faith that it will change. Maybe not as fast as you want, but change happens. Pain and grief do dwindle and wane; the feelings fade as we take a new breath and the next step forward.

It might be helpful to look at an earlier time in your life when your pain was so deep and real. My young daughter will sincerely be sad—her tears are genuine—when she's had a great time with a friend and their play has to come to an end. I comfort her, knowing that the sadness will pass quickly. She does not have the life experience to understand that there will be other times to play with friends. The loss seems so permanent. As we mature, this kind of situation is easy for us to handle. But it is so overwhelming to the child in tears. As we gain life experience, the trick is to remember that it's true of all levels of pain. Don't try to gloss over pain that is real. Take care of yourself, love yourself enough to nurture yourself and accept the love and presence of others who care about you. At the same time, you can know that pain and grief will pass with time.

It is not that we want to forget our pain. Our pain teaches us; it has value. To throw it out is not to honor it. But we must also have perspective about when to allow ourselves to grieve and when to move on. I wish I could give you a formula that would tell you when to be still with the pain and when to let go. I can't. Part of it is trial and error and life experience. And even though I can describe a piece of the rhythm of pain, the experience is different for each of us.

ON GRIEF

Grief is a deep kind of pain, a pain from a significant loss. Grief comes in waves. Relax, know there is a flow, and there will be time to breathe.

As a kid growing up in California, I used to go to the beach to play and swim in the water. I was pretty small when I learned that if I wasn't watching, a wave would knock me down. It's a scary feeling not to be able to take a breath when you feel you need it. The more I would fight the wave, the more desperate I would be for that air. After a while, I learned that if I would relax, the wave would knock me about and when it was finishing, I could just stand up and breathe without a struggle. As I became more experienced, I learned that if I dived into and under the wave, I would not be knocked around one bit; I could come right back up on the other side for air.

It's not a perfect allegory, but perhaps you understand what I'm saying. Even when you feel knocked down or closed in by your grief, IT WILL PASS! It is a wave. And like a wave, it is likely when you are grieving that it will not be just one wave. A wave means there could be another cycle. But while grief comes in waves, they are not of the same intensity. Eventually, healing occurs, through time, faith, new perspectives, love of others. Eventually you will heal.

Some loss is so deep and so wide that it seems you will never heal. The loss of a child is like that I'm told. It is not the kind of loss you "get over." But those who have suffered the deepest losses have found a way to be with themselves and accept. Still, grief will take them by surprise from time to time. This too shall pass. Faith is a great gift to give yourself at times of great grief. To trust that there is somehow meaning, that maybe you can use your experience to help others heal.

Know that everything, whether we understand it or not today, has a purpose in this great universe. This is a place of hope and healing. This is a place for being with yourself and others in a tender and loving way and a place from which, when the time is right—and only you can know when that is—to step forward.

It is so important to allow others to be with you while you grieve. You don't have to be alone in grief. Friends, some family, counselors, even a pet can add to your comfort and healing. Prayer reminds us that we are not alone.

IF YOU ARE WITH OTHERS WHO ARE GRIEVING

If you know someone who is grieving a loss, it is important to be with them. The death of a loved one, for example, has no words of consolation. It is best to sit in loving silence and let the other talk. Resist the temptation to make comments like, "it was for the best" or "their pain is over," etc.

We can't always understand why someone else might grieve over something we view from a different perspective. Maybe we have never been in the position of loss that they are experiencing. These are the situations where the power of silence, and the love you put into the silent space, is profound.

To sit with someone in their grief is to halve it,
to be with someone in their joy is to double it.

ALCOHOL AND DRUG ABUSE: SELF MEDICATION

There are many reasons why people might try to "self-medicate" with drugs, alcohol, and even cigarettes: frustration, pain, stress, boredom, "everybody's doing it." Some people use these substances with the intention of simply partying or having fun. Please don't kid yourself. You should know that poisons in your body have the potential to create more problems in your life than you ever bargained for, and the results may be the farthest thing from recreation.

But let's start with the most superficial of reasons for avoiding the deliberate ingestion of toxins: it can ruin your appearance.

SMOKING

Cigarettes will rob you of oxygen that might otherwise be used to keep your skin nice looking. You've heard all about the damage that smoking does to your body. Ever see anyone dying of emphysema? It's an ugly and very sad thing. But let's get a little more surface here. Smoking makes you look old. Not the mature kind of old that some young people like. As my consultant to this section of the book, Ann Akers (who gives workshops on these topics) says, "Smoking makes you look old like the kind ladies worry about . . . the kind of old they buy the lotions for." Compare the wrinkles (and the voice) of a smoker to a nonsmoker to have a clue about the effects.

Smoking will turn your teeth an off shade of yellow. And it will leave you smelling stale.

One more note: ingesting (eating) one single cigarette is shockingly dangerous to a small animal or child. If it's your choice to smoke, please be careful about where you leave your cigarettes and even the butts.

DRUGS AND ALCOHOL

Drug use can take a toll on your appearance, but that is the least of it. *You* are in the position of power in your life on this one and although there may be a negative fallout to other people in your life, *you* are the one who lives with the consequences of drug use. One challenge with drug use is that *you can accidentally take one dose of something that will change your life forever.* Or you can impair your judgment in such a way that in a heartbeat you find that you have done something stupid that will change your life evermore, irrevocably, everlastingly. No turning back.

Before I launch into a few details, before you make a decision to use or continue using drugs, there are questions to ask yourself: What is your motivation for drug use? There is a list of reasons why someone would use drugs and it varies as widely as people themselves vary. Some of the common reasons:

- boredom (have you fallen for the program that you need to be entertained at all times or have you never been given the freedom or guidance to explore what your real heart's desire might be?)
- to lose weight
- rebellion (ask yourself what you are rebelling against and brainstorm the ways you can really be effective—dig deeper for yourself)
- seeking attention (are there other choices of getting what you need or finding another avenue to fill that for yourself?)
- peer pressure—sometimes real but often imagined (because people talk like they are doing so much, there is an imagined pressure; keep in mind that many people embellish what they do and others are straight-up liars)
- avoiding emotional pain (keep reading . . .)

If you are in emotional pain and want to escape, remember that using drugs will simply shove your problems to the side. There, they will wait for you. While they wait, they will grow. If your problems are like weeds that make you feel as though they are strangling you, keep that train of thought and imagine how much easier it is to get rid of a weed when the garden is tended to earlier rather than later. Hey, not everybody is a master gardener when they start out. So, consult with someone who has experience. There are expert gardeners who know how to rid your garden of strangling weeds. It is not only okay to ask for help, it is brilliant.

Anyway, once you are clear about your personal motivation, once you have some knowledge and information about the reality of drugs, you are in a better position to make a decision about the actions that will serve you.

Alcohol. From the book *Buzzed* (read this book for more on drugs and alcohol!): "For most people alcohol is not a terribly dangerous drug—but it is a powerful drug, and must be treated accordingly. No one would take a powerful antibiotic or heart medication without the advice of a physician. But alcohol is available to virtually anyone who wants to have it, without a prescription. The vast majority of people in the United States face the decision of whether to use alcohol, and how much to use, during their high school or college years. The responsibility for making these decisions falls on each individual."

There are a few basics that I'd like you to know about alcohol. First of all, if you or anyone you know does binge drinking, you need to know that in addition to vomiting and hangovers, in a short time a person can ingest enough alcohol to die. If someone you know passes out from binge drinking, their body is still absorbing the alcohol in their stomach and they can die in their sleep! This is a medical emergency. Get help! May you never learn this one the hard way.

Although there is a lot of talk about genetic predispositions to addiction, anyone can become dependent on alcohol.

More from the book *Buzzed:*

"Studies have shown that even very moderate drinking during pregnancy can permanently hinder a child's ability to learn and to concentrate. . . . It is unlikely that a single drink kills brain cells, but long-term chronic drinking can cause permanent memory loss and definite brain damage."

These facts speak for themselves. Just one little story (no, it's not the one about the kid who died from drinking— I'm guessing you've heard a story like that?): Who's in control anyway? More than one bartender has told me they see people all the time who are clueless about what they look like drunk. "If they could see a video tape of how they act, they would never drink again." Nobody likes to think of themselves as acting stupid.

If you have had a problem with alcohol addiction you would probably be interested to know that sugar sets up the same response in the brain as alcohol. It is not smart for a recovering alcoholic to eat a lot of sweets, since it could increase your desire to drink again.

DRUG CAUTION!

There is something very "kind" about drugs including alcohol. They do not discriminate! They are absolutely neutral about what they do. Drugs (and the people who will sell them to you) don't care if you have money or not. They don't care what color you are, or what your race, religion, or background is. And drugs are not impressed with how intelligent you are. Drugs and alcohol are equal opportunity chemicals. Please keep reading.

There are some very severe consequences to mixing drugs and alcohol. Any drug you mix with alcohol can put you at risk to die. GHB (also known as the rape drug) which is *odorless and tasteless,* is so potent that the weight equivalent to a dollar bill could be an overdose. The old saying of "not taking candy from strangers" is still true.

Where you go matters. GHB can be absorbed through the skin and is sometimes put into empty plastic bottles. If police come to a place (rave or whatever), some people will spray out the drug into the air in order to avoid being caught with it. Even if you have no desire to do drugs, being around a situation like this can put you at risk for getting a dose of something you have no desire to put into your system.

Sometimes when talking about drugs it is hard to look into the future at consequences. It is not hard to find stories of people who did damage to themselves in a short time. Some damage is irreversible.

Some drugs mess with the chemicals in your brain that influence your mood. If you are dealing with any type of depression, you could cause yourself to really dive into disaster with the damage that can be done. There is always a recovery time after any drug use and that can come in the form of depression as well.

If you want more information on drugs, what's what, what they do to your brain, and if they are addictive, read *Buzzed* (by Kuhn, Swartzwelder, and Wilson). Empower yourself with knowledge.

A WORD ON ADDICTION

There may be a million reasons why drugs and alcohol are seen as glamorous. For sure no one glamorizes addiction. The lottery here is that there is some evidence that there are genetic factors that predispose you to addictions. How do you know if you have that or not? No one starts out thinking, "I think I'll be an addict today." Duh. They party on Friday night. Then it goes into Saturday. Then they need a little "bump" on Tuesday. What you should know about the life of an addict is that their lives become *completely* centered around the addiction. Everything they do is about getting the next dose. (Did you see the movie *Traffic*?) This is one lesson I hope you never have to learn the hard way.

JUST SAY NO? PUH-LEEZE

You don't owe anyone an explanation. If you say "no" then that should be enough, right? My expert Ann, who I mentioned above, understands that most people are not comfortable with saying only that. She recommends having a plan. When you are not comfortable saying "no" just like that, have in mind what you do feel comfortable saying. Practice it and have it ready. "I made a promise to myself that I'd stay sober tonight." Or, "I'm on probation with (parents or whoever) and this would really blow it for me." Or, "I'm not feeling very well and don't want to mess with my system right now." Write me and let me know what plans have worked for you so I can post them on the book's website to be available for others to use.

SEXUAL ABUSE

"There is nothing we cannot live down,
and rise above, and overcome."

– Ella Wheeler Wilcox

Note: If you don't think this chapter is for you, please at least have a look at the five stages of abuse and also at the warning signs of an abusive relationship.

As I sit down to write this chapter, I understand that some of you reading this may have no understanding of the depth of pain involved in this kind of life experience; or some of you may know too well just how dark the dark side of humanity can be. In this one short chapter, I hope to say something to you wherever you are with this one. I hope that through these words some of you might be able to step into the possibility of healing past abuse, or stop abuse that is happening presently, prevent potential abuse, and for some of you, simply broaden your capacity for compassion for your fellow who has suffered in ways you should never know.

If you have been sexually abused and this chapter is too intense for you to read, or if it's not what you need right now, come back to it when you are ready. Also, at the end of the chapter there are some resources and suggested reading that might help.

There is a type of abuse, called assault, when a victim is attacked and forced to comply with the threat of violence. I hope you understand that there is a variety of ways that people are invaded and if you have been a victim, my comments on prevention are not here to blame you for what happened. When someone is sexually abused or assaulted, the blame is entirely on the abuser!

For some of you, my hope is to give you the wakeup call you need so that you can prevent the abuse of a predator. Some victims were so small or so helpless that there was no chance of them protecting themselves. But some of you are being targeted right now and you are in a position to keep yourself, and maybe even another, safe by being alert to the reality and through smart choices. Fearful, no. Awake, yes.

Others who are reading this chapter now have an experience in the past, and maybe the present, that needs to heal; your journey is not easy but I want you to know that it is possible. Healing from the trauma of sexual abuse is realistic. And if you are currently being victimized sexually, I hope you can gain the strength to know that you are not alone and you can stop the abuse. I speak a bit harshly in parts of this chapter in the hopes of preventing some pain. For you, please know that I have a most tender place in my heart. Yours is a difficult journey at best, but it is not without hope.

Sexual abuse is present in so many lives that it's important we talk about it openly. During the development of this book one reader, a peer counselor at her school, told me she hoped there would be a chapter on sexual abuse because *half of the kids who come to her talk about this issue.* If this is an issue for you, please know that you are not the only one to have had this happen. In fact, as I learned more in doing the research for this chapter, many people—men and women—shared with me how this has impacted their lives.

UNDERSTANDING

Sexual abuse happens. It happens too often and to too many people. The perpetrators are both men and women, young and even very old, straight and gay, rich and poor, family members, friends of the family, and strangers. There is not one face for predators. Abuse can be violent, but it can also be a seduction—full of mind games, manipulation, and lies, maybe even threats and fear. The victims are male and female. The predators who look for young people to molest fall into two categories: those who look for very young children, and those who look for older victims, adolescents—still too young to have much life experience but whose bodies function like adults. Adults can also fall victim to being sexually abused! Sexual abuse happens to football players and to bookworms. Skinny, fat, handsome, awkward, there are many descriptions of victims.

If you know someone who has been a victim of sexual abuse, your supportive presence is the best gift you can give. If ever there was a situation to withhold judgments, this is it. You can never know or understand all the factors that were involved in any situation. Sexual abuse is not only about inappropriate touch and actions, it can also be about emotional and mental abuse, or the abuse of power.

A big fear for many—and sadly this fear can be based in reality—is that they will not be believed. The majority of victims that we know about are female. The hardest healing journey of all, though, may be for the guys, who often won't speak of being abused to anyone for fear of being ridiculed. And this may unfortunately be a reasonable fear. If you have a friend who confides in you, believe your friend even though it may seem unbelievable, even though you don't want to believe something like that could happen. It is no light thing.

PREVENTION

I mentioned that predators seek both immature and mature victims. They seek both male and female. Their victims can be popular in a group, or people who are mostly alone, on their own. They look for a vulnerability and can sometimes take months to set up and make their move.

I wish I could give you a foolproof formula for keeping safe. There is none. But there are guidelines. Understanding your boundaries is a place to begin. A friend told me about a time she was walking down the ramp of a very quiet train station. A man approached her and got too close. As he moved past her, he grabbed her crotch. She was shocked and couldn't say a word as she pulled away and ran to her train. Now if you knew my dear friend, you'd know that she is quite outspoken, and this shocked silence was really out of character. What she learned from this incident is that if she had been clear about her boundaries in the first place, she would not have let a stranger get so close. This was a situation where perhaps she didn't want to risk embarrassing someone or herself by "overreacting" when he got so near to her in a nearly empty station.

What are good boundaries then?

Please understand that for every guideline below, I can think of a case where this would not have prevented the abuse. So please know, this is simply a place to begin.

Trust your instincts! If something in you says "this is not right," then that is a red flag. Trust what you feel. Change the situation by getting away if you need to. Say something to the person if you need to get things clear. Do what you need to do no matter how much you might feel embarrassed. It's better to feel embarrassed in the wrong place or to let someone else feel embarrassed than to put yourself in harm's way.

A woman once shared a story with me about a dream she had where she realized she was in danger. Shortly thereafter, she found herself in an actual situation similar to the dream. Because of the dream, she felt the danger, and made her move to keep safe. It was only at a later time that she found out the danger had in fact been real; someone else was assaulted instead of her! She could have brushed it away by saying "it was only a dream," but she didn't and she was safe.

Know and keep your boundaries. Know that your boundaries may change from person to person. As you change, so might your boundaries. You might need to check into your instincts to see where you stand about touch. Personally,

I follow the Jewish religious (Orthodox) mandate not to touch members of the opposite sex who are not related to me. Having come from a lifestyle where I wasn't always so clear about boundaries, the clarity this gave was very liberating. No touch, no question. But something happened that made me know it was a right decision. I got to see how my very young daughter, who has seen me refuse (graciously, I hope) even a handshake, was approached in two different situations where she felt empowered to say "no" when touch was not comfortable to her.

Once she was on a field trip to visit a police station when a friendly officer wanted to shake her hand. She did not want to, but he insisted that it was okay, he was a policeman and safe. She *still* refused. The guy did not want to take no (even twice no) from this little girl. Perhaps he was embarrassed because there was a group of us standing there. Whatever his reason for not taking no for an answer, that was his issue, not my five-year-old daughter's. I intervened, explaining that in our family we are teaching that no one has to touch anyone else if they don't want to. He finally backed off.

The second time was with a friend of the family who my daughter had hugged good-bye in the past. This time when he asked for a hug, she refused. He couldn't believe it and expressed his hurt feelings. Meantime, I cheered for my little one for having the courage to say no when that is what she meant. It is okay to say "no" *whenever* you have the strength to do it even if you haven't been able to in the past. It's also okay to say "no" even if you don't think you have the strength to say it. Just saying "no" when you need and want to is empowering.

In business, it is commonplace for people to shake hands. I was mulling over if I should compromise and shake hands in the business world for promoting this book. After seeing my daughter's power from my example (I never could have done that as a kid), my plan is to hold this boundary in place. I am keeping that boundary because it is the right one for me and I am doing it so that you know you are not alone in keeping the boundaries that are right for you.

Stay public. Sometimes you can be with someone you think you know very well, someone you think is safe—a teacher, a coach, a counselor, a religious, youth, or scout leader—but they can manipulate a situation and your trust in sneaky and dangerous ways. If you keep things in public— that is to say, do not be secluded—you increase the odds of preventing sexual abuse. If you are dating, please know that you increase your safety by not allowing yourself to be alone in private with the person you are dating. Groups can be fun. Getting to know someone through private conversation can happen in a restaurant, or a mall, or in the lobby of a fancy hotel where there is no charge to sit on a comfortable couch in a safe environment.

There was a story in the paper about a rape in a military school. The couple were alone and kissing. Things got out of hand. Did the girl "ask for it"? No, there is no justification for what happened. Could she have prevented it? If she had stayed public, a rape would have been much less likely. There is another case of a personal trainer who went for a private session to a man's hotel room. *She had worked with him before and thought she knew him.* It was a painful and costly mistake.

You are not invincible. Oprah interviewed the woman who was jogging in New York's Central Park late at night and was gang raped and severely beaten. Of course the men who did this are accountable, but this woman will never make the mistake of putting herself in such a vulnerable position again. It may not be fair that people need to lose some freedom because of the evildoers in this world, but it doesn't mean you can defiantly close your eyes to dangerous situations with a feeling of entitlement. I'd rather you whine about how unfair life is than suffer the pains of sexual abuse and assault.

STAGES OF ABUSE

The following summary about the stages of abuse is adapted with permission from Dr. Leigh Baker's book, *Protecting Your Children from Sexual Predators* (New York: St. Martin's Press, 2002).

> "Every relationship develops in stages. An abusive relationship also follows a pattern that progresses through stages. When a sexual predator stalks [someone] he or she will use the stages most commonly found in a romantic relationship in order to seduce or overpower a young victim."
>
> –Dr. Leigh Baker

STAGE ONE—DETECTION

In this beginning stage, a predator (think of an animal who is stalking in secret before it makes its move) will search for a victim. *The initial meeting is a critical maneuver because the sexual predator will notice detail that will help him or her evaluate the strengths and weaknesses of a potential victim. And this information is essential for planning a strategic seduction.*

Factors that determine vulnerability:

Your age. The younger you are, the more vulnerable. If you are as young as twelve or fourteen, and even as mature as eighteen or nineteen, and you look and feel mature, you still don't have the life experience of someone who is, say, twenty-six. I'll never argue with a three-year-old who insists he is a "big boy" because for him, he is as mature as he's ever known. He does not have the life experience to know that his perspective and judgment will change. You are at that marvelous in-between age as you lean into adulthood. Don't make the mistake of *feeling* more mature than your life experience is in reality.

Availability. Perhaps one of the most important factors for a predator is unlimited or unsupervised access to you. When you go to any kind of doctor, a nurse or assistant (or friend or parent) should be in the room with you. Any time you are available and unsupervised, please pay attention to the following signs so you can be aware of situations where you might need to protect yourself.

Your emotions! If you are not feeling good about yourself, you are more prone to abuse. If you're experiencing sadness, depression, confusion, feeling abandoned, or if you've recently experienced a loss (divorce or death for example), you are more of a target for a predator.

IMPORTANT: Relationships that are kept secret from other adults are never acceptable. You need to know that when an adult asks you to keep something just between the two of you, or suggests that other adults "wouldn't understand," these are *red flags*. The difference between a surprise and a secret is that a surprise is something that will be revealed. A secret is not okay. The trustworthy adults in your life (even when you're mad at each other!) are there to help protect you. Don't keep secrets from the honorable, responsible people in your life; they are on your side.

STAGE TWO—THE APPROACH

This seductive phase has the predator getting closer to the victim by becoming just what the victim wants. A predator can turn on the charm. They might even meet and gain the trust of parents so that they can spend even more time with you! Wonderful gifts, special time together, saying just the right thing at the right time—a predator will customize his or her behavior!

STAGE THREE—SUBJUGATION (GAINING CONTROL)

Understand that at the beginning of this stage, the controlling behaviors of a predator are slight and easy. It could take the form of *friendly advice, suggestions, reminders, and occasional criticisms*. It is a slow process of getting the victim to get distance from friends, parents, teachers. The predator offers a "special" friendship. The purpose of this stage is to isolate you more and more while gaining more and more control.

STAGE FOUR—GROOMING

Continued isolation from parents and friends, special activities and gifts help gain further control as the predator prepares for the abuse. Here they will experiment with your boundaries by, as one woman calls it, "accidentally on purpose" touching or rubbing in private places. Rewards may come after these kinds of touches. Setting up secrecy is also a part of this stage. One of the other tactics used is to make the victim believe that he or she is "so adult" (and can therefore fulfill "adult" needs). *REMEMBER: If you have to keep it secret, BEWARE!*

STAGE FIVE—THE ABUSE

Here the predator will work at making sure the bonds are strong. Pleading, promising, threatening, or creating fear can all be put to use to manipulate. Guilt and shame are also the tools of manipulation. The predator will turn it around as if the youth created the seduction! Sometimes the victim feels pleasure (which adds to the confusion) and the predator will use that: "See, you wanted it, didn't you?"

Sexual contact that you don't want is not okay.
Sexual contact between an adult and a youth is not okay
—even if they tell you how mature you are!

WHEN A DATING RELATIONSHIP
CAN BECOME ABUSIVE

Most abusive relationships are also sexually abusive. Here are some of the warning signs of an abusive relationship:

- intense neediness

- they tell you that you are the only one who can understand them

- the relationship moves too fast

- one partner showers the other with presents, "love," and overwhelming affection

- unreasonable jealousy

- forcing sex when you don't want it

- forcing you to do things sexually that you are uncomfortable with

- separating or isolating you from your friends

- the relationship is so consuming it stops you from other activities.

FOR THE SURVIVORS

This chapter is intended to give you a place to begin and offer resources in the journey of your healing. Mostly you must know that you are not alone. One of the biggest fears victims have is that they are the only one to have experienced such abuse. But that is never the case. It is so prevalent that whatever has been done or said to a victim is not original. You are not alone in your experience. There are people who understand and can assist your healing in whatever the time it takes. There are others who can meet you in the pain or confusion you are feeling as a result of abuse.

If you suspect you were sexually abused, or if you know you were sexually abused, you can begin your healing journey now. If you are experiencing sexual abuse presently, you can get the support you need to stop it. You are not alone, so do not isolate yourself. Who do you trust? It might feel overwhelming when we hear so many stories about adults in positions of authority who betray that trust. But somehow, you have to find a way to trust yourself and go to the person you think could help you the most. Even if they can't give you what you hoped for, they may a stepping stone in the right direction. If you needed something simple like a pair of shoes, but the shoe store didn't have a pair that fit you in the style you wanted, you would go to another shoe store. If you don't get the support you need, find someone else who can help you. Because help is available.

Your healing is a process of discovery. You can do this for yourself with the help of someone experienced in this area. You can ultimately triumph over the pain with the smallest of steps. We each have the capacity to heal whatever difficulties or hardships we might suffer.

"As a more seasoned therapist, I am much more optimistic now about people's ability to heal fully and to create intensely rewarding and richly satisfying sexual lives after abuse. Experience has also taught me that when people solve their sexual problems, they often improve their self-esteem, assertiveness, and relationships."

–Wendy Maltz, author of *The Sexual Healing Journey*

INFORMATION ABOUT SEXUAL ABUSE

Sexual abuse is epidemic. Research estimates indicate that about one in three women and one in four to seven men have been victims of sexual abuse as children. Adult forms of sexual abuse, such as date, acquaintance, and stranger rape, and other types of sexual exploitation are also extremely prevalent.

Victims of sexual abuse are not to blame. The responsibility for sexual abuse rests solely with the offender.

Sexual abuse is difficult to remember. It is estimated that about half of all survivors suffer from some form of memory loss. It is often not until survivors feel supported and secure that they begin to recall their sexual abuse.

Sexual abuse is difficult to disclose. Because of feelings of shame, embarrassment, or fear, many victims of sexual abuse do not report sexual abuse experiences. Many survivors have endured years of silent suffering.

Sexual abuse has serious long-lasting effects. The trauma of sexual abuse can be at the root of many psychological problems such as depression, anxiety, low self-esteem, self-abusive behaviors, social problems, sexual problems, and food, chemical, or sexual addictions. In addition, sexual abuse has been linked with such medical problems as headaches, asthma, heart palpitations, stomach pain, spastic colon, pelvic pain, fainting, dizziness, and a variety of chronic physical complaints.

Recovery is possible. Survivors can recover from the effects of sexual abuse using steps that involve recognizing effects, dealing with memories, overcoming guilt feelings, developing self-trust, grieving for loss, expressing anger, disclosing the abuse, resolving feelings toward the offender, improving health care, and learning that sex can be safe, healthy, and enjoyable. A variety of resources for healing have become available to help survivors recover. These include books, tapes, newsletters, television discussions, counseling centers, support groups, sexual abuse organizations and conferences.

–Wendy Maltz, *The Sexual Healing Journey*
(New York: Quill, 2001)

For More Support or Information

This information is provided as a resource and does not constitute an endorsement for any group. It is the responsibility of the reader to decide what is appropriate for his/her needs.

BOOKS

Bass, Ellen, and Laura Davis. *Beginning to Heal: A First Book for Survivors of Child Sexual Abuse*. New York: HarperCollins Publishers, 1993.

Bean, Barbara, and Shari Bennett. *The Me Nobody Knows: A Guide for Teen Survivors.* New York: Jossey-Bass, 1993.

Carter, Wm. Lee, EdD. *It Happened to Me, A Teen's Guide to Overcoming Sexual Abuse*. (workbook format). Oakland, CA: New Harbinger Publications, Inc., 2002.

Mather, Cynthia L., with Kristina E. Debye, revised edition. *How Long Does It Hurt? A Guide to Recovering from Incest and Sexual Abuse for Teenagers, Their Friends, and Their Families.* San Francisco: Jossey-Bass, 2004.

SUPPORT ORGANIZATIONS, WEBSITES, & HOTLINES

Remember that finding help and support may mean you need to visit multiple websites or make multiple calls. Be persistent, take care of yourself, and get the help you need and deserve.You can also contact any local rape crisis hotline or mental health centers for counseling.

Remember that websites are always changing so if these links don't work, keep looking. It is best not to rely on internet sites for your source of healing. They can certainly be a great support and a great place to begin. It is not wise to use a chat room or internet counseling; there are people who care online, but it is also a place where predators lurk.

National Child Abuse Hotline
www.childhelp.org/get_help

If you need help or have questions about child abuse or child neglect, call the Childhelp National Child Abuse Hotline at
1-800-4-A-CHILD (1-800-422-4453), then push 1 to talk to a counselor.
1-800-2-A-CHILD (TDD)

The Hotline counselors are there 365 days a year to help kids, and adults who are worried about kids they suspect are being abused or neglected. You can call this number if you live in the U.S., Canada, Puerto Rico, Guam or the U.S. Virgin Islands.

The call is free and anonymous. (The Hotline counselors don't know who you are and you don't have to tell them.) There won't be a charge for the call on your telephone bill if you use a regular phone or a pay phone. If you use a mobile phone or cell phone, there may be a charge and it may show up on the telephone bill. Don't use a mobile or cell phone if you want to be sure your call is a secret.

Please, do not make prank calls to any Hotline.
This will tie up the phones and keep them from talking to someone
who really needs help right away.

VOICES in Action, Inc. 1-800-7-VOICE-8
The Safer Society Foundation, Inc. 1-802-247-3132
Prevent Child Abuse America 1-312-663-3520
Child Welfare League of America 1-202-638-2952

If you are a teen or adult who needs help to stop abusing, you can call
413-268-3096 or go to the website **www.stopitnow.com** for help about
the ways to stop sexual abuse. You can do this!! **1-888-PREVENT**
(1-888-773-8368).

Rape Abuse and Incest National Network
National Sexual Assault Hotline 1-800-656-HOPE   www.rainn.org

Covenant House Nineline 1-800-999-9999
"It's 24/7, it's free, it's for you!" **www.nineline.org**

Pandora's Box
www.prevent-abuse-now.com

For a list of organizations that might help you, check out this
website: **www.peacehealth.org/kbase/shc/shc65.htm**

This website also lists several hotlines and the hours they operate:
www.teenlineonline.org   1-310-855-HOPE (4673)

National Teen Runaway Switchboard
www.1800runaway.org
National Organization for Victim Assistance
1-800-TRY-NOVA (1-800-879-6682)
www.trynova.org

1-800-HIT-HOME
No hassles, just help. Free, 24 hours a day. If you are under 18, a real person will talk to you, tell you where to get help, and help give you hope. No
problem is too big or small.

IN CANADA
Kids Help Phone 1-800-668-6868
www.kidshelpphone.ca/en/
This service was developed for you! Some kids worry that their problem isn't
serious enough or they aren't sure what to say when they call. Our professional counselors understand how difficult it can be to talk about something
that is bothering you. We understand the things that are bugging you. And
we are available day or night.

**If you need immediate assistance, please call
1-800-SUICIDE (1-800-784-2433)**
**If you have just acted on suicidal thoughts,
please call 911 to get an ambulance to take you to the
emergency room for medical help.**

"Suicide victims are not trying to end their life . . .
they are trying to end their pain!!"
– Yellow Ribbon Suicide Prevention Program®

One life lost to suicide is a loss too deep for words. For some people, the pain they feel is so deep and so wide it appears to be unconquerable.

If you are considering suicide, please let my words be close to your heart right now as I say to you: Dear one, do not despair, you are not alone. There is a way out of your pain. You are only one person in the world, but you mean the world to those who love you. Even if you are not in a place right now to know that, it is true.

"The higher something is, the lower it falls. So too, the loftiest revelations are to be found in the lowest places. Therefore, if you find yourself in a place seemingly devoid of anything spiritual—don't despair. The lower you are, the higher you can reach."

–Menachem Schneerson

The dark place you feel is exactly the place for you to search for the spark of light within you. Your pain is the beacon to show you where to direct your healing. The way to heal is to apply your love like a salve to the place inside that hurts. ASK FOR HELP. It's okay to ask for help. There are people who have survived what you are going through. They are looking to find and help you!

HOW DO YOU ASK FOR HELP?

- Go to the resources at the end of this chapter and make a phone call.
- Use the Yellow Ribbon Card.
- Find a friend, teacher, parent, clergy, and ask them to spend time and be with you.

Know that you may not find the right connection on your first try. Keep trying. Some people can't understand where you're coming from. They are afraid or maybe they are just not able to help. Ask and ask until you find the right help.

Know that there are people who care!

Know that the pain will lessen.

Know that healing happens.

SOMEONE WHO CARES

Even if you can't find someone who can understand your pain, you will for sure find someone who CARES.

There are people who have devoted hours of their lives to convince you to hang on, reach out, and get the help you need to make it through to the other side of the pain.

There is a way to break through the pain and get to the other side to see the meaning and purposefulness and value of *you.*

On a seminar, a man held up a hundred dollar bill. "Who wants this?" he asked. All hands shot up in the air. He crumpled it up. "Now who wants this?" he asked again. Again, all the participants held up their hands. Next, he threw it on the ground, spit on it and stomped on it. "And now?" he asked. Still, all hands went up.

He went on to tell the participants that they are like that hundred dollars. No matter how crumpled and trampled that bill became, *it held its value.* No matter how down or dark you *feel,* and even if you don't get it *now,* you are valuable.

Some people reading this chapter have lost someone they love to suicide. *If you are grieving the loss of a loved one to suicide:* It is okay and important for you to reach out and ask for help as you grieve. There are ways for you to heal and ways for you to make a difference. There are whole books written for people like you who have survived such a tragic loss. Reach out. Heal yourself, touch another and in so doing you might help another to heal.

"Hope begins in the dark, the stubborn hope that if
you just show up and try to do the right thing,
the dawn will come. You will wait and watch and work:
You don't give up."

—Anne Lamott, writer

SUICIDE PREVENTION
From the Yellow Ribbon Suicide Prevention Program®:

COPING STRATEGIES FOR TEENS
- Try to be open with your feelings.
- Spend time with family and friends.
- Consider the importance of spirituality in your life.
- Get involved with after-school activities.
- Accept others' thanks, compliments, and praise.
- Plan your future and set realistic goals.
- Volunteer—you have a lot to offer.
- Exercise regularly and eat right! (Chocolate is good!)
- Read subjects that interest you.
- Laugh and keep your sense of humor!
- Do not tolerate physical, emotional, or sexual abuse from anyone. Get help immediately!
- Seek help if you feel overwhelmed or troubled.
- Needing help is not failing, it is simply being human.

WARNING SIGNS
- Abrupt changes in personality.

- Giving away possessions.

- Previous suicide attempt.

- Use of drugs and/or alcohol.

- Depression. Lack of self-esteem.

- Withdrawal from people, especially close friends, family, and/or favorite activities.

- Change in eating and sleeping patterns.

- Chronic pain.

- Restlessness—inability to concentrate.

RISK FACTORS

- Problems with school or the law.

- Breakup of a romance.

- Unexpected pregnancy.

- A stressful family life. (Having parents who are depressed or are substance abusers. A family history of suicide.)

- Loss of security. Fear of authority, peers, group or gang members.

- Stress due to new situations; beginning at a new school, college, or relocation to a new community.

- Failing in school or failing to pass an important test.

- Major loss of a loved one, a relationship, a home, divorce in the family.

- Sexual orientation or identity. Suicide is two to three times more likely for GLBT (Gay, Lesbian, Bisexual, Transgender) youth.

LIFE SKILLS
- A well-known life skill for saving lives in a fire emergency is: "Stop – Drop – Roll." The Yellow Ribbon program teaches another vital emergency life skill: "Stay – Listen – Get Help."
- The Yellow Ribbon Suicide Prevention® Card explains the skill, instructs the person receiving the card what to do, and helps youth when they are faced with this life-threatening situation: the fire inside.
- Another skill is to learn how to couple the warning signs with the risk factors. The combination of these factors increases and intensifies the profile of someone in trouble and needing help.

Yellow Ribbon Suicide Prevention® distributes a card called *"Lifeline."* You can get them for free. Keep one for yourself if you want and pass the rest on to others. You could make a difference for someone else. Use the contact information at the end of this chapter. If you need to use the card, please use it.

AN INTERESTING EXPERIENCE

I have had an experience that not too many people have had. When I was nineteen, there was a misunderstanding and some friends of mine got false information that I had been murdered! Unfortunately, there was someone with the same first name as me from a related organization who had been murdered. A friend of mine in an office across the country heard about it and although she questioned to see if it was me, the answers she got led her to believe it was. She called friends all over the country (and even abroad) who all began to grieve over my death. Someone called my roommate who tried to call me at work several times, but my employer would not put them through to me. They began to think maybe something really had happened to me. I heard the whole story when I got home. It was very surrealistic to me. People were calling me up crying. From my point of view, it had been just another day until I was flooded with this emotion from my friends. They were so happy I was alive! It had never occurred to me that someone would grieve if something happened to me. It was a real eye opener.

Everyone is loved. *Even if you don't feel lovable, the people who love you still love you.*

PEACE

Something caught my attention as I did my research for this chapter. As I read the personal accounts of numerous survivors of suicide attempts, I noticed a pattern. Many survivors reported experiencing a feeling of deep peace settling over them as soon as they made the decision to take their lives. But then, in the actual act of attempting suicide, they were shocked by the sensation of unbearable physical pain. The peace they thought they had found turned into pain more intense than anything they had ever experienced.

What is this peace? Is it an illusion? Or is it real? I believe it is both.

When a person makes the decision to commit suicide, what they are doing is deciding to surrender, to let go of their pain. This is the source of the feeling of peace: I'm going to be rid of my pain. The part of this peace that is an illusion is the part that thinks that ending your life is the way to end your pain. When pain has become so devastating in your life that you know you cannot go on living this way, you can make a choice to end your pain, *without ending your life*. That is the true peace.

Let go of your *pain*, not your *life!*

That place of peace is the place of choice. Here is the choice to choose a new life, one that is free of pain. Sometimes we need to hit bottom in order to make a choice to turn, to rise, to return to who we really are. Sometimes we are so stuck in our circumstances, our emotional reality, our day-to-day life—our *stuff*—that we don't even see who we really are.

Healing pain is partly about letting go, surrendering. Once we surrender, we have to choose the direction of our next step. There is no guarantee that the journey will be easy. What has great value does not come without effort and intention.

If you find yourself in that place of peace, consider that you have made a decision to surrender your LIFE OF PAIN. But please don't stop there. Take the next step and CHOOSE LIFE. Choose a new life, because the potential is always there for you. Always.

Choose life, get help, and never give up!

A dear friend of mine who has survived the darkness of being suicidal shared some poetry with me. What I saw and what I want to share with you is that the darkest, coldest winter does give way to spring. If you're willing to trust that the true you is in there ready to come out, like the butterfly in the story at the beginning of the book, your struggle can bring you back to the beauty waiting to fly.

May you be at peace.
May you be free from pain.
May you find comfort and be comforted.
May you find hope and grab onto it for the promise of healing.

For More Support or Information

This information is provided as a resource and does not constitute an endorsement for any group. It is the responsibility of the reader to decide what is appropriate for his/her needs.

RESOURCES
911
If you have just acted on suicidal thoughts, please call 911 to get an ambulance to take you to the emergency room for medical help. If you're thinking about acting on suicidal ideas, call the hotline numbers below since the 911 operators may not understand your needs.

National Crisis Line (Hope Line Network)
1-800-SUICIDE (1-800-784-2433)

If you are thinking about suicide, read this first:
http://www.metanoia.org/suicide

Girls and Boys Town National Hotline 1-800-448-3000
(TTY 1-800-448-1833)   www.girlsandboystown.org
Call With any Problem, Anytime. Open 24 hours a day, everyday
   The Girls and Boys Town National Hotline is a 24-hour crisis, resource and referral line. Trained counselors can respond to your questions every day of the week, 365 days a year. We can help teens and parents with suicide prevention, depression, school issues, parenting troubles, runaways, relationship problems, physical abuse, sexual abuse, emotional abuse, chemical dependency, anger and much more.

Suicide Awareness Voices of Education
www.save.org
The mission of SAVE is to educate about suicide prevention and to speak for suicide survivors.

For more information on the **Yellow Ribbon Suicide Prevention Program®**, an outreach program of:

Light for Life Foundation International
P.O. Box 644
Westminster, CO 80036-0644
Offices: 303-429-3530   Fax: 303-426-4496
www.yellowribbon.org
email: **ask4help@yellowribbon.org**

IN CANADA
Kids Help Phone 1-800-668-6868
http://www.kidshelpphone.ca/en/
This service was developed for you! Some kids worry that their problem isn't serious enough or they aren't sure what to say when they call. Our professional counselors understand how difficult it can be to talk about something that is bothering you. We understand the things that are bugging you. And we are available day or night.

BOOKS
Blauner, Susan Rose, *How I Stayed Alive When My Brain Was Trying to Kill Me*. New York: Quill, 2003.

Cobain, Bev, *When Nothing Matters Anymore: A Survival Guide for Depressed Teens*. Minneapolis, MN: FreeSpirit Publishing, 2007.

Crook, Marion. *Suicide: Teens Talk to Teens.*
North Vancouver, BC: Self-Counsel Press, 1997.

Nelson, Richard E., PhD, and Judith C. Galas. *The Power to Prevent Suicide: A Guide for Teens Helping Teens.* Minneapolis, MN: Free Spirit Publishing, 1994.

Shneidman, Edwin S. *The Suicidal Mind.* New York: Oxford University Press, 1996.

You Are Never Alone

"Every now and again, take a good look at
something not made with hands.
A mountain, a star, the turn of a stream.
There will come to you wisdom and patience,
and above all, the assurance that you are
not alone in the world."

–Sidney Lovett

This chapter is *not* titled "You are never lonely." You can be at an event with thousands of other people and still feel lonely. As you grow aware of yourself and become aware of your value—just for showing up in this world—loneliness can diminish. If you are willing and open, time will help you grow and you can learn the patience it takes to understand that lonely times will pass. By now you have the idea that you can change the course of things with new choices. In any case, whether you find yourself feeling lonely or not, you are never alone! In a way this might be the most important thing I have to say to you. You have friends seen and unseen. This means there are people who care for you and love you who you can name, and others you are not aware of. Maybe you haven't met them yet. Maybe you never will.

And just maybe some of your friends are heavenly. Even if you don't, won't, can't believe in angels, you can still have the positive emotional and physiological benefits if you imagine that you do. And here is a thought: picture angels who never leave you. Even if they can't intervene they are there to hold your heart and carry your prayers heavenward.

There are many worlds within this world. If you have ever happened upon something you have never been exposed to before, you might look around and see a whole reality that you never considered. There are thousands of people who are involved in different things that are whole realities in themselves. Scuba diving, sports, hobbies, collections, travel, flight, spelunking (exploring caves). Those are just examples of things you can be involved with in the physical world. Every spiritual teaching that I've been exposed to talks of other worlds beyond the physical world that we know. Worlds within worlds.

We have all heard stories about people who have lost someone close to them and yet seemed to receive comfort from that person through dreams or other experiences. I have heard stories about children who seem to have a knowledge of, or even a relationship with, a grandparent who passed away before their birth.

I write this book based on the premise that there is a Creator, Force, Higher Power, All that Is, Was and Will Be, whatever you call her, there is a God. This world is purposeful and meaningful and you matter! Whatever it is that you encounter, do, or feel—you are cared for, you are valued, and you are never alone. The intervention comes in ways and at times that you might not expect, ask for, or desire, but you are never alone.

GOD, How Could You Do This to Me?

There once was a terrible accident at sea that left all but one sailor on a cargo ship dead. The exhausted survivor hauled himself up on the tiny beach of a deserted island. He prayed to God with all his might to be rescued, but no one came to save him.

The days stretched into weeks and the weeks into months. The man filled his days with work, building himself a little hut. He longed desperately to be among people again, but he consoled himself with the work of his hands, and his constant talking to God.

One day, he returned from scavenging for food to find his hut in smoldering ashes, burned to the ground. Everything he had made was gone. "God, how could you do this to me?" he raged. God had abandoned him. He was totally alone, a broken man.

The next day, the man awoke from his tormented dreams to the sounds of a boat: He was saved! Delirious with joy, the man asked his rescuers how they had found him after all this time.

"We saw your smoke signal," they answered.

God is as close to you as your next breath. Know that your simple yet amazingly complicated breath is a gift of renewal and love, and an opportunity. Breath goes to the heart and is pumped to every part of us. Breath can be a reminder to us to live up to who we truly are in every new moment.

HERE'S A THEME
It is not only okay, but important to ask for what you need. Ask for help, a hug, information, encouragement. Ask yourself. Ask your friends. Ask your family. Pour your heart out to God.

HERE'S AN EXPERIMENT
When you are alone sometime—feeling lonely or not—express your gratitude: in writing, in thoughts, spoken words, feelings, song, dance. Whatever works for you.

> "What a lovely surprise to finally discover how unlonely being alone can be."
>
> –Ellen Burstyn

Part Three

You
And the World

"Not everything that can be counted counts,
and not everything that counts can be counted."

−Albert Einstein

REFLECTIONS ON RELATIONSHIPS

"The best thing to give to your enemy is forgiveness;
to an opponent, tolerance; to a friend, your heart;
to your child, a good example;
to a father, deference;
to your mother, conduct that will make her proud of you;
to yourself, respect; to all men, charity."
–Francis Maitland Balfour

"In each of us there is a little of all of us."
–Georg Christoph Lichtenberg

There is a myth floating around that there is such a thing as independence. Being self-reliant is a good thing, but no one can go it alone. We live in communities for a reason. We are all *inter*dependent. We need each other. We provide love and support for each other. We reflect to each other the ways we need to grow. Someone makes your clothes, someone grows your food, someone else built your home, the roads you travel on, the car you drive, and entertainment you spend time with. Someone taught you to read this page.

WE ARE REFLECTIONS OF EACH OTHER

A sometimes very difficult concept is that whatever you see in another is a quality that is within you. It's kind of like the old cliché, "It takes one to know one." Do you think someone is smart, funny, successful, kind, generous, good-looking, or strong? You have that quality in you. If you don't see it there then you need to dig a little deeper or simply allow yourself to see and experience those qualities. If someone is irritating, impatient, or angry with you, it is a worthwhile exercise to dig into yourself to see what that is reflecting in you. Recently I took a deep breath and took a deeper look at someone I felt annoyed with. To my great surprise and relief (even though I knew about this and have done it before, it always amazes me when I apply it), I found that I just might have some of the same characteristics as the person who bugged me. What I was also able to do was understand that it was never the intention of that other person to be irritating. I know when I approach people about things that matter to me, I'm doing it out of genuine caring. Now when I see this person, I am genuinely happy to have a friendly exchange. Does this sound a little too "lovey-dovey-goody-two-shoes"? So what? It's a pleasant way to walk through life. And healthier, too.

Sometimes it's not about exact reflections. Sometimes it's about revealing where we need to grow. If you are in a position where someone is not respecting you for whatever reason, maybe the question you ask yourself is, "How am I not respecting myself?" I dated a man once who betrayed me. I had a choice: I could play victim, "poor, poor me," or I could take a difficult look at how I had betrayed myself. I realized I saw only what I wished he was and not who he really was by his revealing actions. That's pretty dishonest, no? I betrayed myself by settling for something that was not honoring what I *really* wanted in a relationship. I betrayed myself by ignoring the warning signs (including what other men told me about him!) in the first place.

NEWCOMERS

A man was sitting on a fence at the edge of his small town enjoying the sun. Another man walking into the town saw the man on the fence and approached him. "Hello, I'm new in this area, can you tell me please, what are the people like in this town?" The man on the fence answered with a question of his own, "What were the people like where you are coming from?"

"Oh," answered the newcomer, "they were great! It was really hard to leave. We were always doing things for each other and I'm really going to miss them." The man on the fence answered, "I think you'll find the people here to be about the same."

A short while later, a second man entered the town by way of the resident on the fence. "Excuse me, I'm new to this town, can you tell me, what are the people like here?" Again the man on the fence answered with the question, "What were they like where you're coming from?"

"Oh," answered the second man, "I couldn't wait to get out of there. The people were all so grouchy and mean." The man on the fence answered, "I think you'll find the people here to be . . . about the same."

THE ONLY ONE YOU CAN CHANGE IS YOU

"Consider how hard it is to change yourself
and you'll understand
what little chance you have of trying to change others."

–Jacob M. Braude

Echo

A young boy was hiking in the mountains with his father. The boy tripped and fell. Feeling frustrated, he let out a cry. To his astonishment, he heard his cry repeated from across the valley. Frightened that some unseen person was watching him, he shouted out, "Who's there?" Again his words were repeated back to him. Furious that someone appeared to be making fun of him, he raged, "You loser!" The voice accused him right back: "You loser!"

The boy's father knelt next to his son and said, "Listen." He cupped his hands around his mouth and shouted, "I love you!" Over the cliff came the reply: "I love you!" "You can do it!" shouted the father, and again the voice returned the praise: "You can do it!"

"What is that voice?" asked the bewildered son.

"It is an echo," replied the father. "Sounds go out and return to you. It's a lot like life. Whatever you put out into the world comes back to you. So say what you want to hear back again, and give what you want to receive. If you send out love and affirmation, you will be surrounded by warmth and companionship all the days of your life."

If you find yourself reading something in this book and thinking, "I should give this to so-and-so, he really needs this," that is the exact time that you should be paying attention to integrating the lesson for yourself. I remember reading what for me is still a very deep concept, simple but deep: *If you are trying to change other people by telling them how they should live their lives, you are avoiding taking responsibility for your own life.* The moment I was introduced to that, I thought to myself, "I need to tell this to my mother!" I ran to the phone to call her, to tell her that her trying to change me was not taking responsibility for her own world! I had the phone in my hand when it dawned on me that I was trying to change *her*! Hah! I put the phone down.

CHANGE YOURSELF AND THE WORLD AROUND YOU CHANGES

Have you ever heard of Feng Shui? It is the Chinese art of placement. It is a system that works on the premise that your environment influences your life situations. Feng Shui teaches that if you move three things in your home, it will change your life. You can apply the same idea to your:

- behavior in private (perhaps how you keep your possessions or even how you take care of your body)

- actions with other people (the way you speak to others, for example)

- thoughts (e.g., if thinking about the movie you saw makes you feel frightened, think about something else, or if thinking about a certain person always makes you mad, change the way you think about them or direct your thoughts somewhere else!)

- emotional choices (choose writing in your journal over useless worry or anger)

- spiritual choices (add another act of loving kindness to your day, say one prayer, give a blessing, light candles)

It's the same premise. Change what you are capable of changing and it will be reflected back to you. You can't change the world, but you can change yourself and your world: your environment, your thoughts and perceptions, actions, attitudes, expectations, job, friends, plans, goals, clothes, whatever. Those changes will be reflected in the people and experiences you encounter.

WHAT IF YOU WERE 100 PERCENT RESPONSIBLE?

In her book *Living in the Light*, Shakti Gawain asks: "What if you were 100 percent responsible for your relationships, not 50/50 but 100 percent? What would you do differently?"

This is a tricky one because we are taught that both people in a relationship are responsible. It would be worth it for you to ponder and experiment with this one. You might just be astounded by the results. I didn't say this is an easy thing to apply. What is of great value deserves this kind of care and attention. You might find that you set yourself up for better treatment by taking better care of yourself. You might find a relationship improving or a negative relationship ending (which can certainly be an improvement!).

There's a story about a woman who went to her counselor saying how much she hated her husband. She said, "I want to divorce him in a way that will really tear him apart!"

The counselor thought for a moment and then recommended: "Shower him with compliments and indulge his every whim. Then," the counselor added, "just when he knows how much he needs you, you can start the divorce. That would really break him."

The woman took the counselor's advice. Some months later when they ran into each other the counselor asked how the plan was progressing. "Great," was the woman's reply.

"And so you filed the divorce papers then?" the counselor probed.

"No way! Are you nuts?" the woman replied. "We have never been so happy and so in love!"

GETTING ALONG

There are a few priceless techniques to enhance our relationships with the people in our lives:

Give the benefit of the doubt when you can. Giving people the benefit of the doubt is a good way of keeping peace and promoting understanding. This is not about redefining your boundaries, however. It is not about compromising who you are, but rather about choosing the high road. Author Stephen Covey (in his book *The Seven Habits of Highly Effective People*) tells the story of a ride he took on a subway train in New York one day. A man and his children came onto the subway car. The kids were terribly noisy and he was annoyed with the unruly children as were other passengers. After a while, he asked the father of the children—who was not paying attention—to please control his children a bit more. The father quickly apologized and explained that they had just come from the hospital, where his wife, the children's mother, had died an hour ago. Can you imagine Covey's response? "I saw things differently, and because I saw things *differently*, I thought *differently*, I felt *differently*, I behaved *differently*. My irritation vanished. Everything changed in an instant." His heart opened and he offered sympathy and compassion.

The kids were the same kids, but now the traveler had a different perspective and was able to shift from angry to sympathetic. Is there a way you can make these kinds of shifts in your life so that you'll be more comfortable or understanding or peaceful with people around you?

Be forgiving. Forgiveness is not about making another person feel better. It's not about letting someone "get away" with something they did that is out of line. It is not about letting people walk all over you. Forgiving is about understanding the humanity of others and letting go of their frailties and mistakes. Forgiving does not mean you even have to stay around someone who is always doing the same hurtful or irresponsible thing. Forgiving is finding the peace inside of you, the strength to let go of what needs to be let go and to move on.

A popular misconception is that forgiving is done for the other person. The truth is that forgiving is done for *your* healing! Which do you think is healthier, feeling bad or angry about someone, or being able to let go and be free to do and feel in a healthy way?

I know some people believe it is best to forgive anyone for anything. From my perspective, there are some people that we are not necessarily even in a position to forgive. Jewish law, for example, states that you are not in a position to forgive someone who has murdered. The person who is murdered was really the one the crime was perpetrated against so you are not truly in a position to forgive a murderer. The murdered person is really the only one who can do that, and since they are not even alive, how can they?

There are acts that are unforgivable. When we can't forgive, sometimes the best we can do is simply to try to prevent repeat occurrences. We don't forget what happened; we need to learn what we must and teach what we must. But we also want to be sure we stay in balance; we can't let unforgivable, unforgiven acts overwhelm us. Most of us, thankfully, are not in such an extreme position.

For most situations we'll come across as we walk through our day, forgiveness is one of the best healers for ourselves and others.

Forgiving yourself for the mistakes (or at least the perceived mistakes) you make yourself is important. Asking for forgiveness from others when appropriate can also be healing. After we say something mean in anger to someone we really love, an apology can be meaningful. Someone once told me that parents give children the opportunity to learn forgiveness when they make mistakes and ask to be forgiven. It hit home for me. As a parent, I can teach forgiveness by asking for it when I know I said or did something that was not right. As my parents' child, I can forgive them when they make a mistake and say or do something that might have had a sting to it. How about using that same thought in other situations, too? The people who love us want to forgive us, just as we want to forgive them. Taking a first step can be difficult, but when well received is such a relief.

There once was a high priest who would approach people who were fighting with each other. He would tell each that the other had told him they wanted to reconcile. Neither had said so, but the truth was living inside them, because they would often run to their fellow and make peace.

Let time heal your mistakes and the mistakes of others. Time can be a great factor in healing a relationship. With time most of us can grow. With time a needed perspective might come. Time can also reveal the truth about the way someone will come through for you or not in the long run.

One thing for sure: we all make mistakes. Do your best to correct a situation. What are your relationships worth? Ironically, we often make our worst mistakes with the people we are the closest to, because we let down our guard with them. If we get too comfortable, we may say or do things that hurt (or on the flip side, they may hurt us). When we or they or both blow it somehow, the hurt can run deep. It wouldn't feel so deep if we didn't care so deeply. And we wouldn't care so deeply if there weren't love there in the first place. There is a teaching that says, "Better a false peace than a genuine war. "This can be helpful to remember with all of our relationships.

We fall. We get up. We forgive. We let go.
We grow together.

WAKE UP TO THE WARNING SIGNS
Earlier in the book is a chapter on intuition but here is a tidbit more because it is so important.

At the same time that we want to grow, heal, and nurture our relationships, we must also be aware of "red flags"—the warning signs that things aren't all the way right. We want to give people the benefit of the doubt, but we must draw the line when we see danger signs. How often in *hindsight* do people recognize the signals that were there all along? Here are some examples:

- A woman begins a relationship with a man. The man hasn't ended his current relationship. It's no big mystery when he leaves her for another.

- You have an uneasy feeling as you get involved with . . . (You fill in the blank—business relationship, personal relationship, the guy you pass in the hallway, whoever.)

- More than one *reliable* source warns you about a person or a situation.

- Someone tells you something about himself that you are not comfortable with.

- Someone calls you only when they want something from you.

Trust the red flags you spot. Don't explain it away or let a very charismatic person talk you into something you do not want. Pay attention, don't "go to sleep" or go into denial about it.

Even in familiar relationships, when you see someone falling into a destructive pattern, it's important to protect yourself (and anyone else who might be in your care). Sometimes we forgive and forgive because we crave to have those special relationships in our lives. But if that relative with the drinking problem is still drinking, it may just be best to stay away.

ASK FOR WHAT YOU WANT AND NEED

If you are feeling sad and need to talk, call a friend and ask to spend time. When it's time to celebrate, ask for friends to celebrate with you. Just be sure you are giving and receiving in a balanced way. You might be surprised how often you get what you ask for, or at least part of it. Know that the answer may be "no" and you can move on, or let it go, or get what you need somewhere else.

Even in the most intimate of relationships, the people closest to you are not mind readers and can't just automatically provide what you need and want. Ask.

You can also ask yourself if you can give what you need to yourself and let that fill you up. If the answer is no, then ask for help.

Asking for help is part of being human. There are people who have been through any experience you can possibly be going through. You can find someone who knows how to teach, resolve, repair, heal, and correct. There are people available to support you. Whatever obstacles you may be experiencing can be overcome with persistence, fueled by your desire, your willingness, and your intention. Ask for help. It's okay to ask for help! Really. If someone turns you down, that wasn't the right person for you; find someone who says yes. Also know that the help may not look like what you imagined. You may get what you need and want through very surprising channels.

While we're on the subject of asking for help, don't be shy about asking for Divine help, too; no detail is too small!

"It is one of the most beautiful compensations of this life
that no man can sincerely help another
without helping himself."

–Ralph Waldo Emerson

FAMILY

Maturity is doing what you want to do,
even if your parents want you to do it!

PARENTS

Parents are an interesting topic. We all know people who love their parents and we all know people who don't speak (or don't want to) with their parents.

It is your good fortune if you have your parents in the world of the living. Too many people have learned too late that some of the grudges they held onto during their parent's life were nothing more than fragile barriers holding them from the love they really had available. It is so difficult to see that when we are in the heat of disagreement and we forget to look at what is the essential bottom line: Love!

One of the keys in relating to parents is to give them what you wish they would give you. If you want to hear them say "I love you," say it first. Then give them the understanding that they may not be able to express things or give things over to you the way you want. Want respect? It may be hard to start if you're not feeling respected yourself, but if you are respectful, it will come back around to you (unless your parents really have a bunch of other junk going on to cloud their vision, in which case they may really need the extra care). Sometimes it doesn't seem fair, but a "fair" life is not what anyone was promised.

If you want *unconditional* love from your parents but you don't feel like you get it, give it to them first. I know a woman whose parents told her if she married out of their faith, they would not attend the wedding. Most people become indignant to hear a parent make a choice like that. The *unconditionally* loving response is to accept them even when they are not accepting. Some people get love and acceptance mixed up. Just because a parent doesn't LIKE what you are doing, it does not mean they don't LOVE you.

Get it?

That is not to say this is an easy thing to do. But it is so worth the effort, the reaching out, and the compromising it takes. (I'm also not saying to drop all boundaries. It is—as ever—the art of maintaining balance that needs consideration here. Some parents, unfortunately do or say things that are not acceptable—we're talking about extreme stuff here.)

I once heard an interview with a famous director who was asked if his father was proud of him. After a thoughtful pause, he said, "You never get *everything* you want from your parents so you'll have to imagine the rest." This is the heart of what we need to do not only with our parents, but every important relationship. By "imagining the rest," we create the relationship we want inside of us. That fills us up in the way we need and frees us up to acknowledge what is great in our relationships. Now we are in a more whole and responsible relationship on the inside that will most likely be reflected in the relationship on the outside.

Depending on where you are in your relationship one or more of these ideas might make positive changes and give you more of what you want/need with your parent.

Create for yourself what you wish your mother/ father had said and done for you. Be with yourself in that nurturing way. For example, there are people who have, in healing their relationship, taken themselves to amusement parks, bought themselves gifts, written themselves love notes, or simply taken the time to snuggle up with the intention of nurturing the place inside that felt like something was missing. Any action that you believe that a loving parent would or should do for you that never got done is something you can do for yourself. I know people who imagine the conversations they wish they could have.

My friend's parents both passed away when she was fairly young. She once shared with me her sadness that she didn't have her mother to talk with today. I wrote her a letter "from her mother" telling her how proud she is and how beautifully she is living. My friend could have thought I was nuts and out of line. But it was very well received and has become a treasure, not as a letter from a friend, but as if it were really somehow from her own mother. You can write yourself a letter like that, too.

If you can, ask them to be with you now in the way you'd like to have them. My father is not often expressive of his feelings verbally. I asked him on the phone if he would tell me "I love you." For my dad, who comes from a generation of "tough guys" (watch any movie from the forties), it is harder to talk emotionally to an adult child than a very young grandchild. Even though I asked him to tell me what I wanted to hear, it felt wonderful to hear it. I've done this with my husband and kids, too. Sometimes I'm playful or goofy about it; they can't even say some of the things I wish they would. So, I make it up for myself. It might sound something like this: "Oh, thank you so much, Mommy, I love this lunch and it means a lot to me how very much you wanted to make me something I would like that would help me grow and be healthy and strong." A line like that will likely never be given to me by my kids! They simply look at me with a puzzled expression as they begin to eat, and I look at them and lovingly say, "You are so welcome, sweetheart!" A child never really can get what a parent gives until he or she is a parent. A parent, on the other hand, can remember what it is to be a child and take things for granted.

Accept them for who they are, and appreciate what they do right. Hey, everyone wants the great parents from that great TV show or movie. You know, the ones who are always understanding and fair, the ones who always know the right thing to say at the right time. Well, those parents, for the most part, are the really good imagination of the writers. The reality is, there is a wide spectrum of how parents can be with their kids. The majority of parents (they do fall into the category of "only human," after all) do some things very well and some other areas of their parenting are pathetic. We need to give them the benefit of the doubt that they are doing the best they know how. No one wants to have their loving feelings put up for criticism. One dad buys gifts, another one will fix your car, another will be there to talk. One mom gives you sweet cards, another one cuts out magazine articles she thinks will be of interest to you, and still another will always show up for your events. You can look for and appreciate the healthy ways that your parents express their love. You can even look at ways you may not think are so great, and make them into something great.

There is a sweet story in *A Book of Angels* by Sophy Burnham (New York: Random House, 1990) about a woman whose mother was criticizing her. The mother was in the hospital dying and the very conflicted daughter was wondering if it was even worth it to spend the time with her mother if this was what their last moments together would be like. A cleaning lady came in the room and told them how she missed that "mother talk." The mother and daughter were confused as the cleaning lady continued, "My mother died when I was very young and I had no one to talk that mother talk to me." The daughter "got it" in that moment that the criticism was her mother's loving expression.

As always, if a parent's behavior is dangerous, accept reality and get away. Go back to the last idea and create a new relationship within you or find someone to "adopt" that you can spend time with in a healthy way.

Allow room for your parents to grow. Your parents may have made mistakes in the past from their own ignorance/inexperience/immaturity. Who your parents were at your birth, or when you were six years old, or when you were twelve, is not who they are today. They also continue to have life experiences that change them. Chances are they are growing, too, and may be different people today than they were.

Stop gossiping about and criticizing your parents. Just as parents today are taught that children live up to the way you see them, so too, your parents may be capable of rising to the level of the way you treat them. Treat them with the respect they deserve as the people who more than likely want the best for you more than anything else and are doing the best they know how. We talked about how when we create our relationships within they will be reflected on the outside. The way you speak about your parents creates your relationship with them. Experiment with this one. Every time you talk about your parents in a negative way, you are creating a negative relationship within you. If there is only one thing you can change, this is the one I recommend. It's a big one.

Behavior doesn't live in a vacuum. We are in constant relationship with each other. One comment can "push the button" and snowball or escalate tension.

During a time of great difficulties I had with my own mother, we could and often did easily escalate into a big fight. I began to explore the possibilities of changing that pattern. One potentially volatile argument ended abruptly when I said to her: "Wait a minute, let's back up. What you said hurt me; did you mean to hurt me?" Of course she didn't. And I had to own up to her about the hurtful things I had said. We backed up and started over. We've had many occasions to practice the new pattern and be together in a way that is wonderful and supportive. As you mature, you both get to redefine and recreate an adult relationship.

Give your parents their space. Sometimes we kids want to reverse and tell our parents how they should do life. Be with them how you'd want them to be with you. Feedback is one thing, criticism is another.

EXTRAORDINARILY DIFFICULT CIRCUMSTANCES

For a few of you, your parents' behaviors are so harmful and so injurious that it is not worth the risk of being around them ever. (If there was sexual abuse, for example.) It is a natural desire to want the love of parents. Unfortunately, that craving is there even with children in peril from harmful parents. If you have a parent in the dangerous category, it is possible to heal much of the pain and fill the love you need without them in your life! A surrogate parent may help, maybe a teacher or clergy or other mentor. Sometimes journaling or talking it over with friends helps to heal those places. If your history feels severe to you, it is worthwhile to use a counselor or psychotherapist who really knows the healing process. There are many personal growth courses that address some of these issues for healing, too. What's nice about a group format is that you will find you are not the only one to survive difficult or even horrible circumstances. Remember, you are not alone!

If you are currently living in a situation with a parent who is hurting you, ask for help until someone believes you and you can get out. It's true that sometimes things can feel like they are even getting worse for a while before they get better. But things can get better. You can be persistent even if the road is longer than you'd like it to be. If you are a minor, there are many resources for you and there are many kind people if you seek them out. Keep in mind that there are people who will prey on your vulnerability so this is a time to stay alert to your intuition. Here is a good time to apply this one: The best way to get what you want is to say "no" to what you don't want. First, you may just need to know that it is okay to want a safe place to be. (It may take a while to know what safe feels like.)

WHEN YOU ARE THE PARENT— THE OTHER SIDE OF THE COIN

"Kids spell love T-I-M-E."
–John Crudele

I did not have the privilege of becoming a parent until my late thirties. By then, I had already learned so much the "hard way" that when people came to me with pearls of wisdom, I was receptive to listen to what they had to say. The number one thing I heard from people was: "Treasure this time with your kids. They grow up far too fast and then they are grown and gone." Some people told me these are the best times of life, these days of parenting.

Yet, when I was awake with a crying, hungry, wet baby in the middle of the night and surely the rest of the world was cozy and asleep in their beds, I did not feel like time was moving so fast. Time felt eternal while I was sleep deprived. Still, I fortunately had enough life experience by then to consider that there is a big picture, that the people ahead of me on the trail of parenthood knew what they were talking about. I spent every moment I could being conscious that this was a gift I had in my arms.

I found that it was true what I had always heard: you don't really appreciate your parents until you are in their shoes. Who knew that you had to cut tiny fingernails to keep babies from scratching their faces? Who knew that without thinking twice I would step in front of a large diesel truck because my son was too far from me to grab and I didn't think the driver saw my toddler? When you become a parent, you realize that whatever you may have to criticize about your parents, there is more to this job than you ever thought about.

With all of the joy and with all of the challenges of parenthood, it is still something you can prepare for and I recommend that you enter into parenthood aware of the responsibilities. The beauty of it will fall into place and the depth of the gift of parenting will reveal itself in time and in ways that are most unexpected. But first and foremost, you must understand and step up to the reality and responsibility that when you are a parent, you have another life that is completely dependent on you for its survival. A child needs nurturing and attention beyond what you ever thought you could give.

Whether you are reading this from the perspective of a parent or future parent, the number one point, the most important thing I can offer in a few short pages on parenting is this: The most important thing you have to give to your child is yourself. The best way to give yourself to your child is through your time. And there is no time in a parent/child relationship that is not important. When they are little they won't even remember the time you spend, but that is the time that will build who they are and how they relate to the world. When they are big, they may seem as though they don't need you so much, *but they do need you just as much, maybe more.*

Quantity Time

"There is much parents have to teach their children to prepare them for life, love, work, friendship, loss, and death. There is no 'quality time' that can be set aside for sacred and significant communications. It is a continual process of opportunities and surprises, and those memorable moments show up when least expected within a quantity of time spent together. For any of this to work out right, the 'time' must be the ongoing present. That means parents have to be available, aware, and alert. Are you ready to hear that?"

–Dr. Laura Schlessinger,
Stupid Things Parents Do to Mess up Their Kids
(New York: HarperCollins, 2000)

IF YOU ARE NOT YET A PARENT . . .

You may be looking forward to that experience someday. If you are not yet a parent, I have some recommendations for you:

Be sure you are in a healthy marriage. For a child's sake, please consider carefully the consequences of when and under what circumstances you bring a child into this world and whether you are in a position to do so in a solid way emotionally and physically. What kind of environment will you provide for this child? In choosing a spouse for consideration of marriage, you must ask hard questions of each other. Pay attention to the answers. Do you feel the same way about discipline? Education? Religious training? Family time? Although there are extenuating circumstances and not all families can be the ideal, why start out without the best possible solid ground? A mother and father each bring to a family unique gifts that are irreplaceable.

Timing. If you know a teen parent, or someone who became a teen or single parent, you can ask for yourself. Sure, they all love their kids, but they would all say it would've been better to wait to be more mature or in the right relationship.

You must be ready to sacrifice in order to be a good parent. That's just the way it is. You will have to do without some of the luxuries that are available to others to give this little soul what it may need. You will have to sacrifice personal time. As a parent, you cheat your children if you don't spend QUANTITY time with them. The quality will take care of itself in the many, many unexpected treasures that surface in the time you spend. The quality will come up during all the mundane stuff of life, conversations driving somewhere, in the grocery store, or preparing or eating a meal together.

There is no turning back. I remember my dear friend Cathy saying to me, *"When you're a parent, there are no days off, no vacation days, and no calling in sick."* This is part of the sacrifice of being a parent. The thing to keep in mind is that anything worth doing comes with difficulty. Parenting is for sure the most difficult thing there is to do. It is the most challenging, but also can be the most rewarding.

IF YOU ARE ALREADY A PARENT . . .

You might be a parent of a young adult (the people this book is written for) or you could be a young adult who is already a parent. They are different stations in life, but require some of the same understanding. The top of the list is the factor of time. Reread what is written above. All children need your time, they need your attention and availability, regardless of their age.

Beyond that, there are so many books and classes to support parenting. I recommend reading the books and taking the classes as you need them. Use them the same way I recommended this book. Life is a smorgasbord filled with all kinds of information to learn (eat) and integrate (digest). What you are hungry for may have just the nutrients that you need. Experiment with what you learn and see what works for you.

As parents we can never assume that we have achieved communicating to our kids how much we love them. We may think it should be crystal clear to them, from all that we do with them and for them. We may even tell them outright, or give them frequent hugs and kisses. Still, we need to tell them in quiet moments, like when they are getting ready for sleep, when we are spending time during our day waiting for something, during the in-between places.

I do a lot of correcting with my kids. I want them to

"stay on course," so I tell them when they are "off course." They hear criticism, and that must be balanced with good communication and positive talk. Telling my kids what about them I love, how they help me grow and learn, and what is special about them lights up their eyes. They reach out to hug me when they hear these things. It is their way of returning the love they feel in that moment.

Spend time with your kids and communicate what you want them to know.

MARRIAGE

> "Keep your eyes wide open before marriage,
> half shut afterwards."
>
> –Benjamin Franklin

My friend Ethel, a senior friend, told me how much she wished someone had told her when she was young what marriage was really about. Here are a few basics about marriage that you can keep in mind and consider.

The values you live by are the foundation for a lifetime relationship. Know what is important to you and the lifestyle you want to live. Make sure that you share those values with a potential partner. Sharing hobbies or long walks on the beach is nice. When you both love pizza with anchovies or country music, that's great. Even more critical is that you share common values and goals. Do you want to have children? How many? How will you raise them? How do you want to express your spirituality within your family life? What holidays and family traditions are important to you? Sharing a life path will strengthen a lifetime commitment.

Don't marry someone with the hope that they will change. People do grow and change, but they grow from where they already are. If someone is sarcastic and puts you down, it's likely that is the nature of the beast. If someone is loud and likes attention, guess what, they probably always will be that way. If someone is a liar, is that what you want to be dealing with? Pay attention to the person you are considering. What are the qualities that are most important to you now—and if they are not present, move on. If you are clear in your value system or religion, do not count on someone else coming along for the ride. Ask the hard questions first so you know where they stand.

Relationship within a marriage is not a constant. That is the beauty of the commitment of time. Understand that there will be times when you feel closer and times when you feel more distant. There are times when you want to celebrate and times when you want to sleep in.

One of the very precious memories my husband and I share from early in our marriage was both being sick, lying on the carpet like a couple of zombies feeling lousy and weak in our bodies but feeling good in our hearts about the comfort we took in just being together. It is not the kind of dynamic you'll see on a TV or movie screen, but it is the real life comfort of knowing that you are loved and accepted even when you're down and your nose is raw.

On the other hand, it is certain that you will say and do things—hopefully not on purpose—that will hurt your mate. And you will find yourself hurt at times, too. The challenge is to communicate, forgive, and move on. It looks simple on paper. Simple doesn't mean easy. But you get to develop trust in yourself and your spouse as you grow together.

Don't give up on your marriage without deep consideration and plenty of time. Especially if kids are involved. There are several situations when divorce is a positive (even though it may be painful) choice for life: when adultery, abuse, and/or alcoholism/substance abuse is a factor. But for many marriages, there are going to be other things that in the moment feel so huge and permanent that you can't see your way to get past them.

Example: Parenting can be a big area of discord, especially early in parenthood when so much can take you by surprise. Generally, mothering comes much more naturally than fathering. Especially first time fathers can be a disappointment to first time mothers who expect more than they'll get in the beginning. It is my observation that the older the baby gets, the more the father bonds and understands.

One woman I know found that her husband did not rise to her expectations as a new father. She asked him to leave, their marriage ended, and she later confided that she was sorry about her decision. Another friend of mine with a new baby told me she was considering leaving her husband because he didn't seem to bond the way she did. I told her of the other couple and the wife's regret, and suggested that maybe she should give it some time. I shared my experience watching my own husband's delight when the baby started to respond to his voice and then later even say his name (Daddy!). She did give it time and is now in a healthy marriage.

There are other situations in a marriage that just need some time to work out. Even when you can forgive a hurt that you felt from your mate, it may take time for the hurt to heal. Sometimes, it takes time for one of you to find the right words to share what needs sharing.

Keep a sense of humor! If you're the joke leader in your marriage, know when it's good to keep things lighthearted. If you're on the receiving end, keep laughing. Okay, so sometimes it really isn't that funny, but keep your hearts light. A well-placed glassy punctuation with a proper "shocked" expression is always good for a cheap laugh.

Remember the power of your words. And remember the power of other people's words. The way you speak with and about your partner will build or tear down the relationship. Don't talk over your challenges with someone who will put down your mate. Find the support that will help you find the benefit of the doubt or find the words to heal.

FRIENDSHIP

"A mirror reflects a man's face, but what he is really like
is shown by the kind of friends he chooses."

–Proverbs 27:19

If you find yourself in a position to want to make new friends, take a moment and imagine all that you have going for you. If you are not feeling confident at the moment, see if you can let your insecurities have a little vacation. (It might be helpful to read the chapter in this book called "Everybody Has Something" to remind yourself of your humanity and everyone else's.) Tuck your self-doubts comfortably away inside your heart where they can have some TLC (tender loving care), take a deep breath, and find someone you can say a few words to. I can't tell you how many people I've spoken to or read about who were painfully shy, but were perceived as stuck up or snobby. I have found times when I've reached out to someone who was so grateful that I made the first move in a friendship that it took me by surprise. I've had it work the other way, too, when someone reached out to me unexpectedly and opened the door to friendship.

If a friendship doesn't happen naturally over time, my advice to you is to let that be okay. Friendship can't be forced. Everything has its own timing. Trust if a friendship doesn't happen naturally. There are times when I thought for sure that someone would be a good friend and only much later did I understand why it was really for the best that we didn't wind up friends.

Don't rush a friendship. It's like a flower; you can't make it open until the season and the timing is right. Or, like a growing plant, you can't make it grow faster by pulling on the shoots. It needs time, nurturing, and care. Remember: Time is a huge factor in developing friendship.

Cultivate friends who have qualities you admire. Make a list of qualities you want in your friends. Make a list of the qualities that *you* have to offer a friend.

even-tempered	loyal	kind
confident	accepting	deep
honest	happy	lighthearted
empathetic	open	honors privacy
similar values	shared values	good listener

People reveal who they are by what they say and even more by what they do. Author Maya Angelou teaches, "When people show you who they are, believe them." Abigail Van Buren (Dear Abby) taught, "The best index to a person's character is (a) how he treats people who can't do him any good, and (b) how he treats people who can't fight back."

How to Make Friends

A wonderful attitude to making friends is to consider all people as potential friends. If you stay open, friendships can arise from unexpected circles or situations.

- Time, which is a factor in so many other areas of growth, is the next element to making and building friendships.

- Pace yourself—that is, don't expect to become close friends in a week. If you can remind yourself to let go of expectations of how a budding friend should perform, it will help nurture a new friendship along. Start slowly as you and your acquaintances get to know each other.

- Feel free to take a step toward friendship. It's okay to tell others you enjoy their company and that you'd like to spend some time together.

- People like to spend time with others who are confident and comfortable with themselves.

- People also like to be around others who make them feel good about themselves.

When you are making friends, have a look at what attracts you to someone else. It is wonderful to choose friends who will bring out the best in you. It is likely to be temporary if you choose friendship for status.

Friends are a kind of mirror: what do you want your friends to reflect to you about yourself? For sure we are influenced by the people we choose to spend time with. What do you want for yourself and what will your friends reflect about that?

KEEPING FRIENDS

"To have a friend, be one."
–Samuel Herbert

You decide how much energy you want to put into a friendship. If it's not returned, it's okay to let go. When you let go gently, you leave the door open. The welcome mat is out, move on. Here's where giving the benefit of the doubt is helpful. You never know why a friendship is not being reciprocated so don't beat yourself up or the other person. No one ever knows what's going on inside of someone else.

True friends, however, have a way of being with you over time. Sometimes friends are in touch often, daily, sometimes once a year. There is a rhythm to friendships. Like the tide, it flows in and out. As you nurture the cycles of growing friendships through the seasons, consider the following points.

- Accept people for who they are. If friendship is like a living plant, let the friends who are oak trees be oak trees and the friends who are orchids be orchids. Don't expect people to be who you want them to be.

- Forgive your friend when he needs to be forgiven. Give him the benefit of the doubt. We all make mistakes and we all have had the things we say come out wrong.

- Each friend is a whole world. Choose the friends you keep, because who you are around is a reflection of who you are and who you want to become.

- Infuse conflict with patience. Again, give your friend the benefit of the doubt. Sometimes how something is said or heard is not how is was meant. Recently I was comforting a friend and what I said came out all wrong, not how I meant it at all. It took me a while to get the mistake I made and correct it. It has happened to me the other way, when a friend of mine said something that sounded like an insult. When he understood how I heard it, he made the correction right away! You can ask directly if your friend meant to hurt you. Sometimes that is all that's needed to begin healing a conflict. With true friends, you might not even need to ask, just give them the benefit of the doubt and move on.

- A piece of wisdom from a letter written November 2, 1793, by the composer Ludwig van Beethoven: **"When friends quarrel it is much better to have it out face to face than to turn to a go-between."**
  – Elliot Forbes, ed., *Thayer's Life of Beethoven* (Princeton, NJ: Princeton University Press, 1970)

- If conflict is constant, it may be time to reevaluate the friendship and the time you spend together.

- Don't hold on to hurt or grudge. I know this is easier said than done. Let time heal hurts.

- Let go when you need to. There are things that can be done or said that you just don't need to be around, because it's not safe or healthy. Let go. There is a great visualization that works well for this: In your mind's eye, imagine you are standing at the shore of a beautiful beach, put the person you want to let go of on a boat, and send it off with love. Release the boat and the person to sail away. Repeat this as often as needed.

- Consider each friend's capacity and give them the understanding they need. This is about setting your expectations at the right level. Maybe your friend:

    o is having problems at home.

    o is in school full time, has a full-time job and a part-time job.

    o is busy with a new baby—she's sleep-deprived and can't talk for long.

    o is single with an easy job, and lots of time to socialize.

    o is studying for college entrance exams.

    o lost his job and has too much time on his hands.

Since no one really knows the whole story of what's going on in another's life, here is where giving the benefit of the doubt comes into action. Some people are good at covering up depression on the outside. Some people are just not strong enough to resist the flow of peer pressure; they are so afraid of being left out that they betray people they love.

Give people room to grow, change, and mature.

Each of us lives in a world that is ever-changing. Even small, daily experiences of life can move, shape, and change us. A job change, change of residence, a birth or a death, a marriage or divorce all have a profound impact on us. Each day grows into years, and life experience influences our choices.

Again, it doesn't mean if you spend time with someone who is abusive that you should sit and wait for them to outgrow it. Toddlers who bite, on the other hand, will outgrow this behavior with patience and love and not as much time as you think. If you know someone who gossips, for example, and you let them know you don't want to hear it or speak it, they'll either drop you, or respect you and grow with you by not doing that around you. (I've seen this one at work.)

LONGTIME FRIENDS

> "Old friends see the best in us and by that very fact call forth the best from us."
>
> –Black

Acceptance of your friend is the best gift you can give. "I may not agree, but I love you for who you are at your essence."

As you grow and your interests evolve or change, you may need to shift circles of friends. My best advice: do it with love and kindness and gentleness. I learned this one the hard way.

I had a friend of many years. We both felt injured by the other. I blamed her. She blamed me. Neither one of us took responsibility. Oh, the hurt. I still feel sadness and loss for what we once shared when I think of her or when I am in contact with a mutual friend. We were too harsh with each other and I imagine that we would do things differently if we had the chance. It is from the experience of this loss that I learned to be patient with a friend and that time can be a factor in healing.

When another longtime friend said things that hurt me, I was able to take a step back and recognize that she was out of balance. Often what people say is the reflection of themselves more than who they are talking to or about. Even though some of the things she said and did hurt, I experimented with the idea of time as healing and I backed off gently. Although my contact with her became guarded for a while, I did keep in touch. And time, along with her demonstration that this was not a pattern, healed the hurt. My warm feelings returned and we are very close again.

Keeping your expectations realistic for your friends is key. Knowing what is going on in their lives gives you the chance to cut them some slack; when things are rough for you, you can ask for the same. Sometimes. It's about balance again. If things are going wrong often, there is a time to reevaluate a friendship to see if it lines up with who you are and where you are going.

A friend will see the best in you without expecting you to be perfect. A friend sees your weakness and loves you just the same.

A true friend will never expect you to prove yourself or do something you don't want to do. A true friend will support you in being clear and true to yourself. That may mean saying things you don't like to hear in a way that you can accept.

Being a true friend to *yourself* means embracing yourself. It means choosing friends who will be a positive force in your life.

Appreciate your friends! Communicate what you are grateful for, what you admire, and what you value.

I've learned that even when a friend dies, their friendship lives on inside and the love they had for us is sustaining and can continue to nourish us.

FALSE FRIENDS—BETRAYAL

> "Surrounding yourself with dwarfs
> does not make you a giant."
>
> – Yiddish folk saying

The sage Hillel said, "What you do not want others to do to you, do not do to them." That makes sense. To help you keep your personal boundaries, you could also say, "If others are doing to you (or even to someone else) that which is cruel, hurts, creates fear, is illegal or immoral, get away from them!"

I had a "friend" who seemed to come around whenever she *needed* something. But she was never available to reciprocate. Coincidence?

Betrayal in friendship is another chance to see reflection at work. If one is too bold, it shows where the other is too timid. When you see a pattern, you have the chance to grow and create a balance for yourself.

A betrayal of trust is different than a misunderstanding.

It is a serious symptom of someone who does not take the time to consider the consequences of their actions, or doesn't care.

> "No one can make you feel inferior
> without your consent."
> –Eleanor Roosevelt

PEER PRESSURE

There are two main issues here:

- How do you deal with it when friends are doing things that you don't want to do or be around?
- What if you are just different from the crowd?

When people want you to act like them, remember:

> *Not everything popular is right . . .*
> *not everything right is popular.*

When people want you to act like them they have a good, selfish reason. They are likely doing something they know is not right and your behavior will help them justify *theirs*.

THIS IS A TEST, THIS IS ONLY A TEST. What kind of a test? It's a test of your personal strength. Can you stay true to yourself? It's also a test for your friends to see if, when you set a boundary for yourself, they will respect it. It is a test of true friendship. Usually it is a boundary issue even if there is not a lot of drama involved. The very big challenge is that sometimes the test could mean the difference between life and death. Holding firm to what you know is right may get you some flack. The secret here is that it's okay to get flack for staying true to yourself and for staying true to what is right.

Here is another one of those times that I wish I could give you a secret weapon to help you out. There is no formula for when you are in a situation where the people you are with are pressuring you into doing something you do not want to do. What I can tell you is that living inside you is the strength to do the right thing for yourself. Just like with the magic ruby slippers in the *Wizard of Oz* that Dorothy was wearing all along. She always had them with her. I do not need magic to tell you *early* in the story (your life) that you have what you need inside you! Just click your heels together three times and say . . . er . . . I mean, just say what you mean and mean what you say.

When people want you to be like them, remember:

> **"Some people march to a different drummer—
> and some people polka."**
> **–L.A. Times Syndicate**

When people want you to be someone other than who you are, it is a reflection of their own insecurities. It may be time to reevaluate who you are around and why you are choosing them. Some of the most notable people in history, people who have made major contributions, were judged very harshly at some point in their lives. Knowing that may not make the pressure from your peers easier, but I hope you can see it as a beacon of hope to pull you through so you can celebrate what makes you unique.

In any case, when your friends or peers are putting pressure on you that is not supportive or positive, it may be time for you to examine who you spend your time with and why.

Often, people are afraid that if they let go of one thing, even if it isn't working or healthy, it may be their only chance. You can see it all the time when people stay in unhealthy relationships with someone who is clearly not good to be around. You can see it even in work situations: someone stays in a job they hate because they are afraid to take the next step in their life. So it can be with friends. Especially if it is a whole network of friends. I have seen some people make life changes which are very profound, that meant they would have to trust if they let go of a whole bunch of people that were harmful to be around, they would develop new, healthier friends.

> "When the character of a man is not clear to you,
> look at his friends."
>
> –Japanese Proverb

COMMUNICATION

"How often things could be remedied by a word.
How often it is left unspoken."

—Norman Douglas

In my mid-twenties, I got a pretty ridiculous traffic ticket. As a pedestrian, I ran across the street at a green light while the light flashed "don't walk." A motorcycle cop pulled up next to me and wrote me up for jaywalking!!! I had missed the green "walk" by seconds and it seemed unbelievable.

But life gives us exactly the lessons we need.

The ticket was ten dollars. At that time my struggle and hardship meant that ten dollars was my grocery money. I put the ticket away to pay when I got a little more caught up financially. When I did finally send in a check for the ten dollars, I got back a letter that said I took too long to pay, I now owed $171 and I had to appear in court. When I got there, the judge gave me the choice to pay or serve three days in jail. Talk about drama. It then came down to doing community service (but now that I was working full time, I didn't have the schedule for that), or (who knew?) I could actually make payments.

Had I gone to court in the first place to COMMUNICATE, there is a good chance that the ticket would have been thrown out. At least if I had shown up and told them I couldn't even give up ten dollars all at once, I could've bought time or made payments.

The lesson, $171 later: take care of things when they come up. Handle things or they will wait very patiently and force the issue.

I once worked for a small chain of jewelry stores who had their own credit department. The woman who did collections complained to me that if people would just call in, *communicate* that they were stuck, they could renegotiate the payment schedule. She made it sound so simple and easy. It really is that simple. The bottom line here is that if you owe money, you do have to pay it. You don't get to flake out on your obligations. But as long as you show your clear intentions, even with five dollars until you have more, you can avoid bad credit or a bad reputation.

If you have an appointment and you are running late—CALL. No matter how annoyed your appointment might be, it is better than showing up late without the call. If you are not going to show up at all, call. It may not be nice to ditch them in the first place, but it's worse to do it without communicating. Don't avoid it because it may be uncomfortable. Tried and couldn't reach them? Call later and apologize.

The more clear you can be with yourself, the more clearly you can communicate with others, the better you'll feel about yourself, the better you'll sleep at night and the more willing you will be to answer your phone or run into people.

This isn't just for business. Andrew and Tom made a date to go skiing together. Andrew phoned Tom a couple of days later to back out because he realized that he doesn't like to ski in spring. There were no hard feelings, they just decided to do it earlier next season. Honest, simple, clear communication.

When you know an agreement needs to be renegotiated, communicate. It may not feel comfortable and that's okay. You don't even need to give reasons or excuses. You don't have to tell the credit company WHY you can't make your full payment. Tell them what you can do, and do it.

In my undergraduate college, I signed up for a summer session course worth five units. I didn't wind up taking the course but I didn't bother dropping the course either. Instead of the teacher dropping me for not showing up, he gave me five units of fail. I had a great GPA up until that point. All I had to do to avoid losing my honors was communicate. At least I got a story out of it.

DIGGING DEEPER

"The greatest problem of communication is the illusion that it has been accomplished."
–George Bernard Shaw

I have a friend who was in conflict with his mother for years. It was only on her death bed that he finally had the courage to make his peace with her and communicate his love. What

I can tell you is that he is grateful he had the chance to make that connection. I can't tell you how many people I have spoken to who have not taken the time to communicate their hearts to loved ones only to find it is too late.

The most important thing we have in this world is each other. What a waste it would be to find ourselves old, having not spoken the words of love to the people who mean the most to us.

THE POWER OF SILENCE

"Learn to get in touch with silence within yourself and know that everything in life has purpose."
–Elisabeth Kübler-Ross

Silence is not a void. Your presence, your awareness, and your intention are very real, valuable, and powerful for either positive or negative.

- Silence is a statement. The context and intention of your silence determine whether you are healing or hurting yourself or another.
- Silence is an invitation or a brick wall or an expression of love.
- Silence can be a deadly weapon; it can be evil.
- Silence can be a tool in negotiation.
- Silence can give consent.
- Silence can be a righteous act.
- Silence can hold you up in dignity or bury you in shame.

There is a saying that we have two ears and one mouth so we can listen twice as much as we speak.

There are times when speaking out is critical. In the face of injustice and especially in the case of evil, we must speak out. Otherwise silence is an accomplice to evil.

When you are with someone who is grieving, your loving silence is the greatest gift, the most powerful thing you can say. Allowing someone to speak or not speak, as they need, is a gift. Actively listening, silent prayer, a kind or loving intention are beautiful contributions. There is a story of a woman who lost a child—a loss beyond comprehension. At the funeral, many people spoke to her; often their words were awkward at best. One tall, strong man came to the grieving mother and without a word, he held her hand. One of his tears dropped onto her hand. That moment—that silent and very full moment—gave to her more consolation than any words could.

Our silence opens a space for others to explore what has meaning.

"Choose silence of all virtues, for by it you hear other men's imperfections, and conceal your own."

–Zeno

GOSSIP

"For good or ill, your conversation is your advertisement. Every time you open your mouth, you let men look into your mind."

–Bruce Barton

What if . . . when the time comes for you to cross over into the next world (you die), you have to hear every word you have ever spoken? And now you're listening with a "higher" point of view? Will you sit back and enjoy the words you've spoken? Will you get a laugh, be touched, joyful, or embarrassed? This thought occurred to me once while yelling at my son! If you had to "eat your words," how would they taste? How would you like them to taste?

I don't believe it's possible to walk through life without making a mistake with our words.

The principle of not speaking *or listening* to gossip is one of the lessons that changed my life and relationships with people most dramatically. It is one of the hardest and without doubt most rewarding things to be aware of as you walk through life.

Who hasn't been stung by the sharp words of another? Worse than that, who hasn't said words that pierce the heart of another?

Joseph Telushkin in his book *Words That Hurt, Words That Heal; How to Choose Words Wisely and Well* (New York: W. Morrow and Co., 1996), writes: "Even the child who chants 'Sticks and stones' knows that words and names *can* hurt him or her: The statement usually is an attempt at bravado by a child who more likely feels like crying."

Consider this teaching from the Talmud about words. "A person's tongue is more powerful than his sword. A sword can only kill someone who is nearby; a tongue can cause the death of someone who is far away." When someone withdraws a sword to kill, he can change his mind, returning the sword to its sheath. Once words have left your lips, they can never be returned. Killing doesn't only mean physically: words can harm someone's reputation (or their ability to earn an income, or damage a relationship, and more) and the damage can be devastating.

The tricky thing about this topic is that *even something said with no bad intention can still cause damage.* That is why I encourage you to do your best not to talk about other people at all. This is a lifetime process. Just keep on fine tuning the words you speak.

The beginning of my mindfulness of the impact of words spoken even casually and the power they have, came while talking to a friend. She was speaking very kindly about a third person who I know well. Her words were so kind

Yenta

There is a folk tale about a woman named Yenta who went around her village telling tales about all her neighbors. She meant no harm, really, she just had news about everyone. She told the story of one couple who had such good news, they were expecting—it was a marvel because the couple was so old. It turned out they were "expecting" a package in the mail from another country. Then there was the husband who was very poor, saving "a large sum of money" to buy his wife a special gift. Yenta told the story in the marketplace, publicly, where two thieves overheard the conversation and ransacked the poor man's house. The truth was he carried a few coins in his hat band for their anniversary, but the damage to their home would cost them dearly.

It wasn't a long time before the people of the village stopped inviting her over and not long after that people didn't want to talk to her at all. She grew lonely and went to the rabbi for advice. He stroked his beard and thought for a moment before asking if she was really willing to do anything it would take. He asked her to collect stones of a certain size to fill a pouch he gave her, and then return to him.

When Yenta returned, the rabbi poured out the stones to examine them. He took one and angrily threw it behind him right through a window, which broke into many small pieces.

"Why did you do that?" Yenta asked, now trembling.

"Just as this small stone can shatter a window, so too can the words that leave your lips shatter the heart of a friend." He turned to Yenta and told her to return the stones exactly to the places she had found them.

"But Rabbi, that would be impossible, how can I ever remember exactly where they came from?"

"Ah," answered the rabbi, "that is exactly the point! Like these stones, your words can never be put back." Yenta understood and from that moment on she always carried the pouch with the stones as a reminder of her lesson.

that I reacted by trying to give her a "balanced" perspective, letting her know the other, more negative, side of this person. She stopped me cold before I could say a thing. The conversation never took the dive that my reflex reaction began.

I never really considered myself a "gossip," thinking that gossip was only the things you say to hurt someone behind their back. *Merriam Webster's Collegiate Dictionary* (tenth edition) defines gossip as follows: "a person who habitually reveals personal or sensational facts about others" and "a rumor or report of an intimate nature" and "chatty talk." Let me give another way to look at it: If you are talking about someone and it does not directly serve the person you are talking about (e.g., if Julie has a problem, you don't talk about it unless the person you are talking to is in a position to help her) or protect someone from harm (e.g., Joe is known to cheat in business and you tell someone who is talking about becoming his business partner), then you are gossiping. It becomes an even more sensitive issue when dealing with parents or young children, because the potential for harm is even greater in these close relationships. In the case of children, gossip can have harmful repercussions for years! The injury that keeps on giving. (If you improve in only one facet of this, do it for kids.) There are two reasons to stop talking about other people:

- When you talk about someone else you can harm them. Also, you do not allow for the growth and improvement of the person being talked about.

- You hurt yourself and the listener too. Gossip is an ugly thing.

- Understand that if something about another person is true, it is still gossip. Even if you would say it to the person directly, it is still gossip.

"Believe nothing against another,
but upon good authority;
nor report what may hurt another,
unless it be a greater hurt to others to conceal it."

–William Penn

LISTENING

Listening to gossip is the other side to this coin and it is damaging, too. Everyone knows that smoking is harmful to your body. It is also well known that secondhand smoke is just as dangerous, if not more so, than inhaling the thing in the first place. Think of listening to gossip the same way you think of speaking it. Once a teacher stood before a class. He posed this question to the group: "What are earlobes for? Each part of our body serves a purpose, so what is the purpose of the earlobes?" The group sat still with no answer. The teacher folded his earlobes up over the opening to his ears as he said, "So you can cover your ears if someone around you is gossiping."

How do you get out of a situation when someone is gossiping and you don't want to hear it, yet you don't want to sound "holier than thou?" Here are a few ideas that I've successfully employed. Experiment depending on the situation and the person you're talking with.

- Walk away.

- Change the subject or redirect the conversation.

- Be up front and explain that you don't want to listen to conversation about someone else.

- Say with a smile, "I also won't listen when someone wants to talk to me about you."

- If someone is upset and needs to vent some steam, know inside you that the person speaking is out of balance. Don't assume anything said is even true. Maybe you can help the person venting give the benefit of the doubt to the other.

Once people understand that you don't engage in gossip, it pretty much stops coming around. But trust me, there will always be an opportunity to practice this one and fine tune it as you go. Remember, though, if someone tells you something that lets you know they or someone else is in harm's way, it is a good thing to tell about it to someone else who is in a position to help them.

So, what do you talk about? What do you listen to?

"Talk is powerful. Speak bad about someone and you
expose all the ugliness in him, in yourself,
and in whoever happens to be paying attention.
Once exposed, the scar begins to fester and all are hurt.
Speak good about the same person,
and the inner good within him, within you,
and within all who participate begins to shine."
–Menachem Schneerson

Be Nice

"You cannot do a kindness too soon,
for you never know how soon it will be too late."
–Ralph Waldo Emerson

My high school horticulture teacher, Mr. Koubatian, used to put a quote on the board each day. One that really stuck with me: "You can catch more flies with a teaspoon of honey than a gallon of gall." (He spent some time, in memorable detail, explaining that gall is the bile that the gall bladder produces.)

As I begin this chapter, I'm on a plane to New York. My plans had glitches that were corrected by my asking for things *nicely!*

I used a special mileage bonus award to get a free flight. It needed to be booked three weeks in advance. Since I was trying to coordinate this trip with a very busy friend, I waited to hear from her to complete my travel arrangements. I got it all figured out just in the nick of time, but the operating hours of the service I had to book through were shorter than I realized. I missed my deadline to book the flight for free.

The next morning, I explained my situation to the operator with a gentle question about any available inventory for the day I wanted to travel—two weeks and six days away. After putting me on hold a short while she came back and told me: "You know, we never do this, but you were so nice. I don't even check when people are rude to me, but I got you in . . . What time . . .?" Talk about direct feedback. The woman on the line told me loud and clear that it was my nice approach that made the difference.

Please know, being pleasant is not about going overboard or being a phony or what some call "saccharin"—fake sweet. People know when you are not for real. On the other hand, if it is not the way you were brought up, you can "fake it til you make it." That's not the same as being phony, because your intention and desire to be a kind person is real and it counts.

When you are nice, it will more often than not be reflected back to you.

People who work in outside sales are taught it is important to be pleasant to the receptionist of the purchaser or they might *never* even see the client. Imagine the salesman who was terribly rude to the secretary only to discover she was the boss's wife! You never know who is related to who.

When it is hard to be nice, be nice anyway. In the long run, you will never look into yourself and be disappointed for being compassionate or gentle.

"The world is not a reasonable place.
Meet it on its own terms:
When you do something good, do it beyond reason."

–Menachem Schneerson

I want to note here that being nice does not mean you don't keep boundaries or that you say "yes" to every request. It is perfectly acceptable to say no graciously and set limits. When necessary, say no. Do it nicely when you can and if nice isn't understood, go for firm. Being firm is not the same as being rude.

MAKE A POINT TO BE KIND

Open a door, give someone your seat, compliment a stranger. Kindness is the extra little bit that you can make a point to do. I encourage you to experiment. Compliment a child and take a moment to bask in the warmth of the smile you get. (Please, do it with a kid you know or at least make eye contact with the parent so they know your efforts are sincere!) You can find something nice to say to anyone, even if it is only, "I like your tie."

There is a bumper sticker that says, "Practice random acts of kindness." Try putting some money in the meter of someone about to get a parking ticket. They will never know you or that you did it. You will feel good about yourself. (Who knows, maybe someone has done it for you?)

Lift your heart, lift the hearts of others.

What about when someone is rude to you? What if they are miserable? I once felt frustrated with a cashier because she was rude with me. I asked her, kind of sarcastically, if she was having a hard day. Thank heaven she didn't know I was sarcastic. I saw her shoulders drop in relief and she answered me, nearly in tears, that it had been a terribly hard day for her. I shifted before she finished her sentence and was in real compassion. Who got the blessing in that one? It was a profound learning. The more you can remember to be compassionate, the more you will notice people smiling at you when you need it most!

The more you lift others, the more you are actually giving to yourself. If what goes around comes around, why not start sending around more kindness? It's a great experiment and I'd like to hear how it works out for you.

> "Kind words can be short and easy to speak,
> but their echoes are truly endless."
>
> –Mother Teresa

BE CLASSY

Good manners are the ground rules of being nice. If you have good manners, people will enjoy being around you.

> "Manners include far more than what happens at the
> dinner table and individuals who do not possess them
> suffer a great disadvantage."
>
> –Zig Ziglar

Do you use the "magic words"? Please and thank you, of course, are really not magic. The *power* of these words, however, is real, influential, and true! Said sincerely they hold even more power!

What about when someone is less than kind to you? What if they are rude and obnoxious? Then what? Should you outdo them and get one up? What do you think my answer will be? Class is responding to bad manners with good manners!

- Be sure you are kind to yourself.
- Do get away from a volatile situation if it is really dangerous.
- Be the person you want to be around: pleasant, agreeable, likable, delightful, good, admirable, excellent, good-hearted, compassionate, humane, benevolent, sympathetic, gentle, friendly, generous.

"Wherever there is a human being,
there is an opportunity
for a kindness."

–Seneca

FEEDBACK

"To avoid criticism, do nothing, say nothing, be nothing."
– Elbert Hubbard

Feedback is nothing more than a reflection of where you are. Feedback gives you information so you can decide if you need or want to change direction. It could be the direction of your actions, choices, perspective, anything. You know the quality of life you want to live. You know you want to be true to yourself. The way you determine if what you are doing is taking you where you want to be is through feedback, which the world will generously supply. Are you paying attention?

Pin the tail on the donkey or piñata, the children's party games, both require blindfolding the player. What makes the game so amusing is that the player has no idea where they need to go. They get feedback—"higher, lower, left, right"—to help them stay on target.

Some people use the word "criticism." Criticism has a negative feel to it, as if the person who's giving criticism has the intention to hurt or put down. And sometimes people do criticize in a way that's hurtful. If you can frame it up in your own mind that it's all just feedback, a neutral tool you can use for yourself, you might find benefit from all the many things that come your way.

Here's an example of how the same feedback could be taken in different ways. You are in school (or work) and no one wants to be around you. Doesn't sound so good, does it? But what if the crowd that's avoiding you is all doing something that goes against who you are? Perhaps it's feedback that you are who you want to be, that you are strong. On the other hand, if you are different than the crowd, in religious belief, skin color, politically, whatever, rejection from a crowd might give you feedback about where you want to look for friends—in a place where acceptance for the individual is open. No one wanting to be around you could also mean that you have some characteristics that are difficult to be around.

Imagine you're sitting in a restaurant with a group of people and someone next to you leans in and whispers, "You have something stuck to your teeth." What do you do? Do you start rubbing your teeth with your tongue and whisper back, "Did I get it?" Or do you snap, "Why are you always criticizing me?!"

Remember the example of the rocket sent into space which is off its course more often than it is on its course? How do the people know it is off course in the first place? All the monitors and gauges they use give them information—feedback.

The key here is to pay attention to what is coming your way and why. Feedback can help you evaluate whether you are on course toward being your best, healthiest, and happiest. If you are getting the same feedback over and over about something in particular, it may be worth listening to. Then again, it may be worth strengthening your resolve about something important to you.

CONSIDER THE SOURCE

It might be worth it to listen to the feedback you are receiving in the world. It might be wiser to ignore it. You have to evaluate the source of the feedback and then consider if it is right for you. Everyone has an opinion. You can listen to as many of them as you want, but you have the final say in what counts, what is important to you, what will support you in moving in the direction of becoming and doing what you want.

Feedback can come from a life situation (you win an award for an achievement) or nature (you're ice skating on a pond in winter and you hear a cracking sound under your feet) or people (what they say and do). You can get feedback directly in ways you can clearly understand or indirectly in a roundabout or subtle way. Feedback can be unsolicited— the kind you didn't ask for—or you can ask for it. You can get it from a source that cares about you and is trustworthy or you can get feedback from someone who doesn't really have your best interests in mind and is simply self serving or manipulating you.

- Who cares about you most? Who has your best interests at heart?

- Who around you is honest, has integrity about what they say and do? (People who lie in one situation are likely to lie easily in others.)

- Is the source of your feedback neutral? (If someone is giving you a sales pitch and they make a commission, it is not neutral.)

ACCEPTING FEEDBACK

When someone is giving you feedback, it's a natural reaction to feel defensive. Say thank you anyway and then sit with the information you got for a bit. It might just be that this is information you need even though it's hard to hear. If you find that there is something there for you, you can decide what to do about it. Sometimes we don't think the feedback we get is right. So we let it go. But what if you keep getting the same feedback over and over? It might be time to take a hint.

GIVING FEEDBACK

The guideline for giving feedback is to "do unto others." Give feedback with the same sensitivity that you'd like to receive it. It is helpful to ask the person you want to give feedback to if they even want to receive it. Something like, "do you want some feedback about that?" is pretty direct. If they say no, honor that no matter how much you know the feedback would be helpful. Asking first shows respect and that might just open the door a bit more to understanding. Or maybe not. "Do not do unto others as you would not have them do unto you" is the other version of that saying. Do not insist that you know better; there are many paths up the same mountain. Don't be attached to someone else seeing things just like you do. Put it out there and then let it go.

"Do not remove a fly from your friend's forehead with a hatchet."

–Chinese proverb

SEX

"Happiness is different than pleasure.
Happiness has something to do with struggling
and enduring and accomplishing."

–George Sheehan

Okay, here it is! Take a deep breath and keep breathing. This is not a "how to" chapter; rather, it is about "why, why not, when, and with who." This is what I wish someone had told me when I was young. The main points of this chapter are not about the dangers of being sexually active (although I do touch upon them, because they are serious and real). Mostly I want to talk to you about heart and soul matters here, how sexuality affects you deeply. The main issue at hand is understanding and respecting the power and beauty of intimacy. But let's start with the physical.

PHYSICAL REALITIES

When I was young my mother told me (I'm paraphrasing here):

Mom: "Don't have sex before you are married."

Me: "Why?"

Mom: "Because . . . you just wait . . . Oh, my father would have killed me."

This was the common belief of that generation. But for me, hey, this was a different time, right? I found interesting books from the peak of the sixties that gave me another opinion: "If it feels good, do it." I listened to music which joyfully sang things like, "if you can't be with the one you love, love the one you're with." Birth control pills were rather new on the market giving women the same "no worry freedom" as men. I read other books which spoke frankly about sexuality, and were very clear about choices for birth control, and also about sexually transmitted diseases. In the sixties and seventies, the worst thing people faced was venereal disease. It had a deadly reputation in history, but today we have antibiotics to knock venereal disease right out. Then there was herpes: no cure, a big drag, but not life threatening.

Of course, if you don't treat sexually transmitted diseases fast enough, they may cause permanent impairment of fertility (which means it will be hard to have babies when you are ready)—or outright sterility (which means loss of the ability forever to have a baby). In addition to potentially losing the ability to have a child because of venereal disease, the risk of certain types of cancer increases with multiple partners. For women, herpes could someday endanger your baby and could actually cause you to have a C-section (where they surgically remove the baby to keep it safe from a herpes sore, which could cause a baby to go blind, or even die!). For anyone with herpes, at the very least it's extra baggage you have to carry around for a lifetime.

Of late, AIDS is the big deal. And even with all the publicity and public service announcements, if you haven't personally witnessed the life slowly and painfully draining away from someone, AIDS may seem to you like nothing more than cold statistics—nothing compared to the warm body pulsing with desire right next to you on an otherwise lonely night.

Then there is the issue of pregnancy! We are not trained to understand that in the heat of a moment of passion, we may pay a price so steep and real. Childbearing and rearing is one of the most wonderful, mystical (although difficult) experiences this world has to offer, AT THE RIGHT TIME!

Pregnancy irrevocably changes your world. Do not kid yourself into thinking that the method of "pulling out" the penis before ejaculation will prevent pregnancy or can indeed be accomplished even with the best intention. Understand that conception can happen the first time you have sex even if you don't climax or reach orgasm. Understand, too, that no birth control method is a guarantee. If you are a woman and you get pregnant, you will always carry that baby in your heart, mind, and soul—ready or not. If you are a man who gets a woman pregnant, you are most likely not going to be in control of the decision the woman makes. You may find yourself a father, ready or not, and linked forever with your child's mother. The men who think they can run from the obligation of fatherhood are fooling themselves because they are ultimately responsible for their absence. Give a baby up for adoption—a noble option for an unwed young couple—and you will always wonder.

There is so much controversy about abortion. You may feel a certain way about having an abortion today, but as you grow, as life experience deepens your understanding, you may not feel the same way about a decision like that later on. Having an abortion will not slip from your memory like the shoes you can't remember tossing out. These issues are real for both men and women. This issue is much more intense for women because their connection is more direct. Men can and do run away from this one, although as I said before they are ultimately responsible for the consequences whether they face them or not.

Sexually transmitted diseases, impaired fertility, death, pregnancy. There is a lot to sort through.

Unfortunately, there is not enough attention paid to how sexual intimacy affects your emotions, or what is going on spiritually! So, let's set aside parenthood, disease, and death, which are hard to comprehend anyway unless you have direct experience.

There are real issues right now that touch you—no Russian roulette about these issues.

WHAT ARE THEY DOING?

Sexuality is plastered on billboards and magazines. The advertisers that use sexuality to sell you a product have no interest in your well-being. Just keep your money coming to buy the products. Keep the machine going. They play into the ever-loosening trend. Pay attention, look around. Is it not ridiculous to use sex to sell food and clothes? I was reading a popular women's magazine and saw an ad for some hair product. My then five-year-old daughter asked me why the lady was naked. "To sell the shampoo," was my response. She thought it pretty ridiculous even at five! It is also a shame that only a certain body type is promoted as beautiful. If you like to think of yourself as someone who can think for yourself, it might be a great exercise to walk through an art museum and look at the many faces and shapes of beauty.

What about pornography? I said this wouldn't be a "how to" chapter but I must say here that if you think a porn film is a good way to learn the "how to" stuff, please consider the following. Many of the people involved in making these films need to take drugs before they go in front of the camera. The people you see in those films have serious issues going on to do what they do (e.g., a reaction to sexual abuse). Often they are depressed or desperate or have a low self-image and think they can't do anything else. Pornography is very disturbing, not because of a negative judgment about sex, but because watching porn is watching very numb or very sad people. You won't learn how to make love from watching pornography. You won't learn the art of being intimate from a pornographic film.

Even on mainstream films and television, if there is a scene that includes nudity, it is always a "closed set." That means that only the people absolutely necessary to the filming can be present. Why all of a sudden this "modesty" from the actors?

What are your thoughts about why advertisers and the media constantly use sexuality to sell their products? Do you think it sets up a healthy system for the way people think about themselves and others? What meaning do you want sexuality to have in your life?

PAY ATTENTION TO YOUR INTENTION

First, I want you to answer this question. What are you seeking when you consider or engage in physical intimacy? Relief? Pleasure? Happiness? Togetherness? Intimacy? Love? Closeness? Acceptance? Bonding? Worthiness? Validation (that you are attractive, desirable, manly or womanly, "in the know," or mature)?

Who and what are you looking to attract? Why? What is the big picture of who you want to be, not in the future, but right now?

You need to ask yourself the hard questions and give yourself the most honest answers. Get real and honest. You're doing this for you. The mind is very clever. We are so good at rationalizing what we want to do that we sometimes are not so honest with ourselves. Can you open your perspective to see life as a whole?

Only you know if you are being deeply honest. Even if you think you're deceiving a potential partner, you're only fooling (and hurting) yourself in the long run if you're not honest about your thoughts and feelings, your perspective and intention.

SPIRITUAL AND EMOTIONAL REALITIES

When you take a close look at a human being, it is hard to separate out the parts we are made up of: mind, body, emotions, and spirit. Books have been written on using humor to heal cancer (the influence of the mind on the body) and changing your diet to overcome depression (the influence of the body on the emotions). Studies demonstrate the effect of prayer on healing (the influence of the spirit on the mind, body, and emotions). All the parts interact and work to change the whole. If you can grasp that all the facets of a person are so deeply interconnected in so many ways, it is easy to see that there is a mental, emotional, and spiritual connection to physical intimacy.

SO, WHAT IS INTIMACY ABOUT ANYWAY?

The English poet Shelley wrote, "Soul meets soul on lovers' lips." On the other hand, Heinrich Heine wrote, "Oh, what lies there are in kisses!"

Of itself, sexuality is neither good nor bad. Fire, too, is not good or bad. Used with respect and understanding of its properties, it can be harnessed for great use: warmth, cooking food, beauty, and comfort. Used without regard and respect for its power, it will burn and destroy.

Here, I must make an important point: SEX DOES NOT EQUAL LOVE. Sex is the mechanical act of body parts coming together. The relationship and intention behind the physical coming together contribute to the setup of positive or negative experiences. In the cases of sexual assault or sexual abuse through seduction, the effects are damaging. When a couple has made a lifetime commitment, the expression of real love through coming together in this intimate way is bonding and can be healing and nurturing and wonderful. So, when I use the term intimacy, at its best it encompasses the physical, emotional, and spiritual *knowing* of the other.

In the ancient text of the Hebrew bible, one of the words used for sexual intimacy is *"knowing."* An interesting thing about *knowing* something is that whatever words you use to describe what you *know* are always inadequate. You can describe the taste and texture and temperature of ice cream, but only experiencing it lets you really know what it is.

Intimacy carries with it huge potential. *Merriam Webster's Collegiate Dictionary* can help us understand a little more by looking at the root word "intimate": *"1 a: intrinsic, essential b: belonging to or characterizing one's deepest nature 2: marked by very close association, contact, or familiarity . . . 3 a: marked by a warm friendship developing through long association b: suggesting informal warmth or privacy . . . 4: of a very personal or private nature."*

Consider what it is to be intimate with someone on an emotional level. Same or opposite sex, an intimate friend is someone with whom you feel safe to be yourself, someone you can cry and laugh and grow with, someone who brings out the best in you and can let go of your mistakes.

> "[W]e kiss . . . And it feels like
> we have just shrugged off the world."
>
> –Jim Shahin

On a very deep level, the experience of intimacy between a man and a woman produces the sense of having "arrived"—there is no place else to go, no past, no future. It is a sense of connecting with the Source of all. It is this "light-filled" experience that people quest for. It is truly nothing less than a spiritual experience. We take the physical and elevate it to the spiritual. But for the experience to have real value, it has to happen in the right relationship and at the right time.

"Is it any wonder that this area, when sensitively and spiritually entered, has the power to build a depth of relationship which is indescribable, and is it any wonder that this is where life is generated?

And is it any wonder that a non-spiritual generation damages this area above all else? If the animal is loosed in this sacred zone, if human depth and sublime understanding are eliminated from this fragile zone of wonder, if the unique privacy and modesty which belong here are damaged, then there is no spiritual in the world of flesh . . ."

–Akiva Tatz

Anything of value requires effort. Building trust, commitment, sharing goals. Physical intimacy is not a path toward emotional intimacy, but it can certainly be a strong glue to binding a marriage. (I use the word marriage here even though some people would substitute "committed relationship" because in most cases, a marriage is a commitment made in front of witnesses with a public accountability. At its best, a marriage is nurtured and supported within a family or community.)

More questions to ask yourself: What is the quality of life you seek? What are you willing to do for yourself to create it?

PRACTICALLY SPEAKING

Some people think, "Well, I've already 'done it' so what's the difference if I just do it again when I feel like it or when the person next to me feels like he or she wants to? It's already a done deal." The truth is, the more relationships you engage in, the more you are potentially hurting yourself.

There are the physical risks and dangers I mentioned earlier and there is an emotional price to pay as well. There is a story about a couple who was standing before their family and friends exchanging their wedding vows. The man said to his bride, "I give you my whole heart." At which point a woman stood up from the group and said, "No, you can't give your whole heart, I have a piece of your heart." Then another woman stood up and said, "I have a piece of your heart, too . . ."

I trust you are mature enough to know that you will not always feel the same way about things as you continue to mature. There will certainly be some values that are strong throughout your life. But we keep changing, growing, and hopefully, getting wiser as we go along.

In their essay "Buying without a Test Drive" (about marriage without premarital sex!), Marc and Beth Firestone note that:

"[C]ars tend to drive the same over time. Parts deteriorate and need replacement, but a Cadillac will always be a smooth ride, and a Ferrari will always be fast. Not so with people. Even if you do a 'test-drive,' five years into marriage your sex life will most likely be very different from that 'test.' Time, age, and experience change a person. As an individual changes, so do their relationships. In a good marriage, as trust grows, love multiplies."

A suitable couple might decide not to marry based on an unsuccessful test-drive. Yet that often bears little resemblance to how their intimate life might have evolved into in a healthy marriage. In fact, it may be that the absence of commitment, mutual trust, and enduring love are the very factors that contribute to a failed 'test-drive.'"

It is okay to say "no" even if you have already said "yes." Whether it's with someone you have never been with before or someone you have already been intimate with, you have the right to change gears and be true to yourself. If you are actively involved with someone and suddenly tell them you now want to wait, a true love will wait with you (even if the first reaction to your announcement is not what you hoped).

"Virgins by choice" are people who have decided to take themselves back. They are people who realize that even though you may no longer be a technical virgin, you can still take control of your body, heart, and spirit through abstinence. You never have to feel bad about being rejected or rejecting someone else. The boundary is clear and if someone else doesn't like it, then you get a sense about who they are and where they are coming from. Your vision becomes clear!

SETTING YOUR BOUNDARIES

Healthy sexuality is about boundaries. If you choose to make your boundaries clear, you have control over the limits you want to set. Here is another place you have to ask yourself the hard questions. What kind of relationship are you seeking? What kind of boundaries do you need to feel safe? To feel good about yourself?

Understand that when you set a boundary that includes touching and "steamy stuff," your perspective can get clouded. One way to keep the channels clear—and this may not be what you want to hear—is by keeping your hands off of the heat. And keeping the hot hands off of you. How many songs have been written about the dreamy, steamy stuff of touch? Touch does not keep your head clear about the person you are with. Looking into his or her eyes and talking about what is important in life—goals, values, dreams—will reveal more than that magical touch and delicious kiss can hold.

There are ways you can control the boundaries. Desire, modesty, and commitment are some of them. Keep reading.

Master of the Master

The story is told about a wise man who frequently went into a desolate forest far from the noise and tumult of civilization. There he would strive to obtain mastery over his thoughts and actions. A king traveling through the forest met the wise man.

"What are you doing in the forest?" asked the king. "What country are you from and whose subject are you?"

"I am the master of your master," replied the wise man.

The king was taken aback by the wise man's reply.

"Explain yourself," demanded the king.

"Impulses and desires rule over you," the wise man explained, "and you are a slave to those desires. But I am a master over them. When I stay here in solitude in the forest, I strive to conquer my desires; hence your master is my servant."

–Kol Tzofayich

DESIRE

Are you the master of your desires, or are your desires master over you?

There is no question that the pull, the desire for physical intimacy is real and strong. It's supposed to be. And it's wonderful—in the right time and with the right person. IT IS WORTH THE WAIT. In fact, the waiting makes it even better and richer. There is an insidious myth at large today that being sexually active makes you mature. No doubt that the experience of intimacy is something you can only know from experience. But intimacy with the wrong person is something you can never take back.

There will always be someone who will very eloquently try to convince you to engage in sexual activity. It may be an advertiser, it may be a friend, and (the most difficult of all) it may be the very attractive date sitting next to you.

MODESTY

We have all heard people say that we want to be loved for who we are. Men complain about women caring for the car he drives or the type of job he has. Women complain that men are only interested in good looks. Yet despite the complaining, in an effort to attract the attention and affections of the opposite sex, many people believe they need to flaunt what they have. But going around showing skin or cleavage or a "six pack" will backfire more often than not.

If it is true that "the eyes are the windows to the soul," then it is precisely the eyes that we want to speak with. If you want people to know who you are, why cloud the essence of who you are and draw attention to what does not really represent you? No matter how the shape of your body changes over time, no matter how your skin will show its age as the decades progress, the sparkle in your eyes can remain bright.

I know more than one woman who made a shift from showing a lot of skin to more modest dress. It's true that the degree of attention decreases, but there is a new, genuine, more fulfilling attention that shows up in its place. The attention is really on who she is, the essence, the personality of the woman.

A fourteen-year-old developed young woman I know was wearing a short, tight skirt with a slit just inches away from her crotch. I (being bold and often outspoken) flapped open the skirt and asked her what it was she wanted people to notice about her.

When I was studying martial arts, there was a man in the advanced class who reminded me of Clark Kent and Superman. He dressed kind of nerdy and he was extraordinarily kindhearted, but when he stepped onto the mat, his strength and poise was revealed. A woman who is only after first appearances would miss that hidden gem.

I trust you understand that dressing modestly does not mean you have to look bad or dull. Look around and watch people. Look in different settings. Modesty is not just the way you dress. It's the way you carry yourself. Not strutting around like God's gift to mankind, but understanding that you *are* a gift from God and honoring that. Like everything else, there is a balance. Modest does not mean timid or weak or bland.

COMMITMENT

Don't mix up loving yourself—filling *your* own needs—with

loving another. Your emotions cloud your intellect. You may already know this from firsthand experience. We have an amazing ability to create relationships in our own mind that have little to do with reality. This can actually be healing and helpful in another context, but in the daily reality of intimate relationships, it can be dangerous.

When you bounce in and out of relationships, you are desensitizing yourself. Each time you "go with someone," then break up and move on, you make it a little easier to let go of the next one and the next. Do you want to practice "breaking up" so you can get good at it? Or might it make a marriage stronger if you didn't give yourself an easy out? If you knew that you would go into a marriage with the strength to really commit, do you think it might make you keep your eyes open and choose wisely? Do you think developing the quality of discernment and commitment would make you more desirable to a partner who has those same qualities? Become—develop the qualities of—the person you want to attract!

A NOTE TO THE WOMEN

I feel sad about writing this, but if I'm going to be true to my original intent to tell you the truth, I must include it: There are men (and a few women today) who see their date as nothing more than a conquest. They would never admit it—maybe not even to themselves. They will, with an earnest face (and maybe even an earnest heart if they cannot be honest with themselves), tell you how much they love you. A seventeen-year-old I know shared with me about a good friend of hers who, after *months* of going out with a young man became intimate with him. He broke up with her the *next day.* She is heartbroken, since from her point of view she "waited" for "the right one." Her pain will diminish with time, but the error in the action she took affected her deeply.

This story is not unusual. Men who are mature enough to be past this kind of behavior will tell you the truth about "chasing the conquest" if you ask them. For some reason fathers and brothers and other men in our lives are not sharing this information so readily. Ask them directly. We want to be able to hold our men in high regard. Bring out the highest in men by holding out the deepest in you for the right time and the right person.

I want you to understand the concept that the people in our lives are a mirror reflection of what is within us. If you are a woman who is being taken advantage of time and again, it is time to step up to yourself and take care of yourself. You teach people how to treat you by the way you accept, allow, promote, and create relationships. This is an important area to be awake to. If you find yourself being betrayed by someone in a relationship, how are you betraying yourself by being with that person in the first place? If you are being abandoned, how are you abandoning yourself by choosing men who will not commit to marriage?

Ladies, you are your own gatekeeper. No one may enter the majestic realm of your soul without your permission.

"Reveal your soul appropriately."
–Laible Wolf

I want you to empower yourself with self-knowledge and self-love and the strength to say "no" when that's what's right or, better yet, not to put yourself in a position to have to fend someone off. By keeping dates public, you keep yourself safer.

Understand, if you seclude yourself with a man in a private place, it signals that you are interested in him whether you mean it that way or not. (It is in these kinds of situations that you become more vulnerable to date rape.) Sometimes even going somewhere public may be picked up as a signal. I knew a woman who went out with her college professor for a drink. She was shocked when he tried to kiss her. She forgot to look in the mirror and notice that she was an attractive woman. She was used to "teachers" keeping their professional distance.

Things change when womanhood blossoms. One woman I know, who had her daughter at age eighteen, wanted me to tell you that "men will say anything to get you in bed. Sometimes girls sleep with a guy because they are lonely and he's saying what she wants to hear. When the guy leaves her, it's lonely on top of lonely."

Men are simply not connected the way women are to the emotional aspect of physical intimacy when performed outside of marriage! Once a man makes the commitment *within* a marriage, intimacy becomes a strong element of building and takes the relationship to depths that only time and faithful commitment will reveal.

It may sound distant to you now, but I want to talk about your "biological clock." It's common for young women to think they have plenty of time, so why not just hang out with Mr. Wrong for a while? I can't tell you how many women I know who are scrambling with fertility issues because they waited until their thirties to get married. When you are young it's impossible to imagine yourself in another stage of life. Here's where the life experience of others can come in handy.

What is it you want in this precious life of yours? Are you looking for someone with whom to build a life and a family? Your womanhood is not defined by how many men are attracted to you. You are not a mature woman based on having a boyfriend. A real woman understands her own nature and honors herself, treats herself and others the way she wants to be treated. A mature woman will set her boundaries and understand that if someone is not honoring those boundaries, it is a test, revealing the nature of the trespasser.

Waiting for (and ultimately finding)
the right life partner is worth the wait!

A NOTE TO THE MEN

It's difficult not to think of sex when you have found a source of desire and pleasure and the world around you bombards you with images of strength and power in relation to the women you can attract. But I'm here to tell you that your manliness is not defined by how often, how many, and how long. Manliness is really defined by how you can stand up inside yourself and conquer your own weaknesses. A real man is someone who takes responsibility for his actions, can admit and learn from his mistakes, and moves on from there. A real man has integrity, understands the importance of his word, and keeps it.

When women around you are dressing in revealing ways, when their behavior is flirtatious and their hands are all over you, in some ways it is harder for you to set boundaries because you might be accused of not being man enough. But remember, you are the only one you have to prove anything to. Although random experiences may seem titillating today, you are the one who has to live with the memories you create. If you can imagine yourself in the future looking back on your life, what is the kind of vision you want to have?

Although you do not have to deal with the same issues as women regarding intimacy, there is still a cost to being sexually active. That cost is really your self-respect. Sound funny? You know very well that the women are the givers of sex and the men are takers. You can't build self respect if you are simply a taker. I have spoken to more than one man who chose (after having been sexually active) to wait until marriage for further sexual intimacy. The way one man put it: "The woman had all the power on a date; if she wanted sex, there was sex. If not, not. Now we are on equal ground."

In a healthy marriage, there is a give and take that is different; you are giving yourself to the marriage, so there is reciprocity. Loving is when both partners are giving to each other. (Lust is the empty taking.) There is a building of trust and depth of feeling that cannot be attained in a night, or month or even a year of relationship. You have to let go of the potential of all women for the reality of one actual woman.

A male friend gave me an example of this special marital connection with this story. A man took his wife to see the doctor about her foot, which had been bothering her. The husband said to the doctor, "We came in to see about my wife's foot which has been hurting us." What resonated for me about this story was something my mother said to me about my father (at the time of this writing they have been married fifty-nine years!), "When he's in pain, I feel it." Can you even imagine the kind of bond that can only grow with a commitment and time?

One more thought that I heard a minister say at a wedding to the couple getting married: The grass is greenest where you water it.

HOW DO YOU KNOW?

How do you know if it's the right person?

First, you need to know yourself. Take a realistic inventory of who you are, what you value, and what you want in life. Make a list of the qualities you seek in a life partner and make a list of the qualities you have to offer as well. I'm not talking looks or likes. If you are inclined to write a description of the way the person should look—hair and eye color and the like—you are not thinking deeply enough. If you are worried that the other person should like the same sports or hobbies or TV shows as you, you are also not thinking deeply enough.

I knew a couple who were married for nearly twenty years. Their whole relationship was based on the business they ran together. When they finally sold the business, they looked at each other and realized they had nothing in common! Another couple I know were both deeply spiritual. They had different religions but thought that it wouldn't matter since they both believed in God. That marriage failed also because once children came into the picture, they had a conflict that could not be resolved.

Finding someone who is just like you is not the goal. Finding someone who will recognize and bring out the best in you and for whom you can do the same is wonderful.

Notice this paradox. On one hand, as people grow, they change. On the other hand, they do not change. The basic personality traits of a person stay the same. You can even look at young children and get a clue about who they will be as adults. If you see a five-year-old who is empathetic and understanding, chances are that's what she'll be like as an adult. If you see a child who is ambitious, chances are he will always have that characteristic.

The wise thing to do is look for someone you like just the way they are. If you think you can go into a relationship and change your partner, you will meet with disappointment. Women, do not look at a man's potential when you make a decision. Men, do not think a woman you need to rescue is a good choice.

As you explore the possibility of choosing a partner:

- Look around you and find several marriages you admire
- Talk with the couples who have a good track record that you want to emulate.

- How did they make their decision?

Spend a long time talking with a potential partner. A five-hour phone conversation is a long phone conversation, but is not enough to justify living together.

If you are young and seeking marriage, you may not have the life experience on your own to have good judgment about a prospective life partner. It is wise to learn about a person's family background to understand more about them. You don't just marry the person; they have a whole family and history attached. You may even want some advice from people whose judgment you trust who are more experienced than you.

How do you know if it's the right time?

Did you ever hear the old song, "Breaking up Is Hard to Do?" *Thinking* that it's the right person or time and having an error in judgment can cause you some heartache. Okay, so you can get past the pain and move on, but how often do you want to do that to yourself? On the other hand think about what you would value more, the thing you worked and saved for or the thing that was handed to you with no effort on your part?

Consider what you value in life. What is important to you? How do you want to honor yourself and a partner? Do you love and respect yourself enough to hold out for what you truly want? Does your partner love and respect you enough to walk through the process with you waiting for the right time? If there is any doubt in your mind or guts, for sure it's not the right time.

Anyone can say they have a commitment to you. They may even think they mean it at the time. Demonstrating commitment is a true test.

I understand that going against the mainstream of popular thought and media that says "just do it and get it over with" is a difficult position to take. Understand that the choice of sexual intimacy has some of the most immediate consequences within the spectrum of choices you can make. I am suggesting that you consider your own heart, mind, and soul first and foremost. In the end, you have to live with the choices you make.

Part Four

Gaining Altitude

"The conqueror and king in each of us is the
intuition, knower of the truth, of the life, of the future.
Let that knower awaken in us and drive the horses
of the mind, emotions, and physical body
on the pathway which that king has chosen."

–George S. Arundale

Because You Are Noble and You Can

"There are glimpses of heaven granted to us
by every act, or thought, or word,
which raises us above ourselves."

–Arthur P. Stanley

In so much of this book I have written about stepping into your highest potential, becoming your truest, best self. Life is an incredible journey, a gift that needs to be acknowledged and recognized. We are always improving, growing, rediscovering who we are.

And yet, in each and every moment, we are given the opportunity to rise, right now! We will always be put to the test. In this very moment, I can choose, fresh, what direction to move and who I am. The past certainly has an influence, but the present moment—the clarity of the deep breath you take right NOW—will determine more than the past. It is amazing how you can recreate yourself with your choices.

Right here and right now is your challenge to rise. Having

read the chapter on gossip, did you—even one time—decide *not* to say something you might have in the past? That is you rising inside yourself in a noble way. This is especially true when you are the only one who knows what you did. The harder it is in a given situation to hold your tongue from saying something hurtful, for example, the more you've risen into your own dignity.

Once a dear friend of mine was talking to me about a situation in her family. She felt that she was the one who was having to be mature for the umpteenth time in the face of challenges. She asked me, "Why do I always have to be the one who keeps it together?" I responded to her, "Because you are noble, and because you can."

So I say to you, dear reader, you too are noble. Find the nobility within you; live in that place. Because you can. Even when it's not so easy. None of us can do life alone. Use the support available to you. Even when you don't know what direction it will come from, it will show up if you look for it.

Rise. Like oil floats on water, let your nature be that of rising to life's challenges. And if there is a time when you feel that you cannot rise, find a safe place to talk it through, or get a paper and write it out. Spill the negative thoughts onto paper, burn it if you need to, let it go, and rise. And when you fall—as every human does—here's the chance to forgive, and then get up again. Rise, grow, wake up, stand up, climb, ascend. Because you can.

> **"Do not let what you cannot do**
> **interfere with what you can do."**
>
> –John Wooden

FORGIVENESS

There is no way to live life without saying or doing something that will hurt *someone*. It happens with people we hardly know and people we love. And there is no way to get through life without getting hurt.

Okay, so hurt happens. Part of the process of dealing with hurt is evaluating where you keep your boundaries and how you hold them. It's also important to examine how you might have participated in a situation that caused pain. Here's when you ask yourself: For which parts can I take responsibility? Did I live up to my commitment? Did I honor my boundaries or the boundaries of others?

It is crucial to drink plenty of water!

What?!

Are you awake? Are you with me? It is crucial to be forgiving.

Think of your body. Without air, water, and food, you will not survive. Love is like air. Although studies have been done on this, I won't cite any of them. If you are reading this book and you are human, you don't need science to tell you that love is an important part of life. Keep breathing. Keep loving words and behavior for the people you love and for yourself, too. If you need to move to a place where the air is better and cleaner, you can do it. Keep breathing.

If love is like air, then water—the fluid we need to survive, to keep things healthy and flowing—is like forgiveness. For our own health, we need to forgive others the hurt we feel. We need to forgive ourselves and others for mistakes.

There are some deeds that seem unforgivable. Even in extreme situations there is a place where forgiveness will heal you. Even if that means forgiving *yourself* for judgments you have against yourself for being a victim.

Forgiving is the thing you do. Imagine yourself even wanting to want to forgive someone and the process has begun. Read that last sentence again if you need to. The desire to want to forgive—even if you don't feel capable at this time—begins the healing process of forgiveness.

Take a deep breath because forgiving is not always an easy process. It does get easier with practice, however.

You don't even need anyone else to be present for forgiveness to work, to do its magical healing. Write your own prayer of forgiveness to say before you go to sleep. Ask for Divine help in forgiving where you need to forgive. In a safe place, let yourself open to the healing ability of forgiveness. Make your desire for forgiveness as wide as you can make it. Say it out loud. Make up a song (goofy is fine, it doesn't have to be radio-worthy; this is for *your* healing) about forgiveness and sing it to yourself.

Please know that forgiving does not mean taking down boundaries. It means letting go of hurt. Starting clean inside of you. Be courageous in your *desire* to forgive and see if your thoughts and feelings change for the better.

WHEN YOU NEED TO ASK FOR FORGIVENESS

The other side of the coin here is making an apology. Sometimes it's simple: "I'm so sorry I stepped on your toe." Asking forgiveness can also be very humbling: "Will you forgive me for my mistake?" There is nothing wrong with getting humble and owning a mistake. We do make mistakes. Sometimes they are big and painful. Owning up to our mistakes with the intention to do better next time (and then really doing better next time) is very healing between people.

Sometimes apologies can backfire, however. I've been in situations where the person I was clearing the air with took the opportunity to put me down and blame me. It gave me a deeper insight into who that person was and how much I wanted (not) to be around them.

When it's up to you to make the apology and the person you are approaching does not want to forgive, try again. Three is the magic number here. If you sincerely try to apologize and after three tries you are rejected, you can know that you did your best and it's up to them.

A FINAL NOTE ON FORGIVENESS

- Forgiveness is one of the most potent and healing forces available.
- There is a difference between forgiving and trusting. Forgiveness can happen even if continued trust does not!
- In some situations it's relatively easy to get past hurt. When it's harder, do it anyway.

Have a long tall glass of clean, clear water and imagine you are forgiven and forgiving.

"... You don't have to have the other person's cooperation in order to forgive them. That other person doesn't even have to know. They do not have to be sorry. They do not have to admit the error of their ways. Forgiveness is about you, not them."

–Dr. Phillip C. McGraw

LEND A HAND

"I don't know what your destiny will be,
but one thing I know;
the only ones among you who will be truly happy
are those who will have sought and found
how to serve."

–Albert Schweitzer

True happiness—for yourself—is found in your service to another. Sound funny? My experience has led me to understand that there is a consequence for every action you take. In this case the consequence is a reward. Even if the reward does not come in a form that anyone else sees or recognizes or acknowledges, it is still real. Feeling good about yourself, knowing you are walking a path that is giving, is a reward in self esteem that cannot be learned in any school or given with any decoration.

When you give something of yourself—time and energy—to help make some little corner of the world brighter, you are lending a hand, you are being of service.

Some people are drawn to a career that is service oriented. You can't really separate the work obligations from the service. Showing up (these positions don't necessarily have high pay), and especially showing up with caring, is a form of service. Volunteering is the most obvious opportunity for putting a piece of yourself into the world and making your difference.

Being of service is one of the more miraculous things you can do in this world. It can be as small as a smile, kind word, or gentle touch. It can be as large as a lifetime commitment, and anywhere in between.

The essence of what I am saying is that there is no giving in this world without receiving. When you give yourself, your time, talent, attention, and love, these gifts will flow back to you as water flows back through a fountain. It could take the form of building a strong character within yourself. Or learning a life lesson that serves you. Or knowing the joy, honor, and humility of the connection between one soul and another. It is said that there is a reward for service in the world to come. If that is true, then what rewards we experience in this world can only be the tip of the iceberg.

You can choose from many forms of service. Experiment with your time and you will surely discover parts of yourself and the wonders of this world.

Step up and do what moves you to make your positive mark on this world, to weave the color of your thread of humanity into the tapestry of life and add dimension to the gift of life.

Don't limit your thinking about what you can do. What do you love to do naturally? Run a marathon (fundraising)? Play chess (spend time with seniors)? Sing (be with kids at a children's home)? Computers (create a web site for a nonprofit organization)? Somehow you can apply your interests and gifts to some kind of service.

Here are a few of my favorite ideas you can try:

- Teach/take classes with the Red Cross (they'll train you!). Know that the knowledge and skills you learn or teach may save a life!

- Tutor an adult in reading. Adult illiteracy is a shameful secret for too many people who for one reason or another didn't get the skill as a kid. Contact your local library—they can train you, give you materials, and match you with someone.

- Hammer some nails. Contact Habitat for Humanity to help build lives.

- Volunteer at a hospital and hold newborn babies who are addicted or have AIDS or are otherwise abandoned by the women who gave birth to them. Sometimes babies are not abandoned, but cannot be attended to by their mothers the way they wish they could.

- Take a class in clowning and walk in a parade or visit children in need.

- Be a big brother or sister. CHANGE THE LIFE OF A CHILD through love, acceptance, and time together. We take simple things for granted, but for some kids just running errands with you gives them something they don't get in their lives.

- Make sure a lost child is reunited with his parents.

- Donate blood. It takes a short amount of time, only a little discomfort, and you may help save a life. And they usually give you cookies!

- Donate money. Even if you only have a dollar, one-tenth of it, your dime, will make a difference. If you only have ten dollars, your one dollar will make a difference. Bring your money to a food bank so you can even see where it is going. Or take ten dollars and buy a fifty-pound bag of rice at a warehouse food supply and donate the rice.

Get out of your own world and step into the world of another soul. The unexpected reward is that while you are "helping" someone else, you have grown and deepened and discovered a beauty, a splendor, within you that you cannot tap into any other way. I don't mean to romanticize this. Take it in perspective because you may not feel great every time you do some service or another. You may feel taken advantage of, or you may come up against your shortcomings in a way that is uncomfortable. You may leave feeling exhausted and unacknowledged. But the work is done! It is like a time-released capsule—the fruits of your labor WILL continue to blossom!

REMEMBER: You don't have to do something on a large scale. You know what your commitments are and what you can do. Start small, but start. Do not underestimate the power of acts of loving-kindness and how those actions can impact the world!

"How wonderful it is that nobody need wait a single moment before starting to improve the world."

−Anne Frank

If you sit down at set of sun
And count the acts that you have done,
 And, counting, find
One self-denying deed, one word
That eased the heart of him who heard—
One glance most kind,
That fell like sunshine where it went—
Then you may count that day well spent.

–George Eliot

You've Got to Stand for Something

"You've got to stand for something
or you're gonna fall for anything."

–John Mellencamp

This chapter stands on the foundation that there is good and evil in this world, that what you do and do not do, what you say and do not say, tips the scales in favor of good or evil! You count and you matter.

There is a haunting story by Shirley Jackson called "The Lottery." Most of the story gives us the setting of a nice little town where everyone knows each other. We get to know the friendly people, who are preparing for a great annual event. Everyone is excited about it. Everyone is looking forward to it. It is only at the end of the story that you realize that the town has been collecting rocks and drawing names for the lottery because the "winner" of the lottery is to be stoned. The woman who is chosen, suddenly terrified as the first stones hit her, cries out for the town not to do it. But people just need to get it over with to get on with their day.

BE WILLING TO TAKE A STAND

What are the ways that we witness injustice in our world and remain quiet because it is not aimed at us? We can sit comfortably in our homes and watch the latest horrors on the news, then flip the switch for our favorite sit com. I'm not saying that we have to spend every waking moment creating justice in the world. I am saying that if something is in your face, don't ignore it. If someone is telling a racist joke, don't just give a sick chuckle—speak up.

What are you about? What are your values and where did you get them? What are you willing to do to back what you believe in? When do you need to take a stand for something and when should you let go of a fight?

Your participation in this world either by doing or not doing makes a difference! There is a Talmudic teaching that says, "It is not your duty to complete the work, but neither are you excused from it."

> **"Indifference is the twin to evil."**
> **–Annette Lantos**

Weigh up what it is that you stand for and what you are willing to sacrifice. Some fights are worth fighting.

In "A Tale for All Seasons," a story by Kurt Kauter, a little coal mouse talks with a wild dove about the weight of a snowflake. The dove tells the mouse that a snowflake weighs "nothing more than nothing." The coal mouse then tells about the time it sat on a branch and watched and counted the snowflakes until at last, with one more snowflake, "nothing more than nothing," the branch broke off. Perhaps, thinks the dove, only one person's voice is lacking for peace in this world.

> "Never doubt that a small group of thoughtful, committed citizens can change the world. Indeed, it's the only thing that ever has."
> –Margaret Mead

KNOW WHEN TO TAKE A STAND AND WHEN TO LET GO

There is a true story about a man whose father worked in a very high-powered industry and had a high income. One association cheated him out of an enormous amount of money. He did battle in the courts with the company and it took many years. In retrospect, the man said he would not have begun that battle and traded his life's energy for the lost time. The time lost to the fight—which could have been spent watching and participating in his children's lives—was irreplaceable.

In first aid training, you learn that there are three times when delay can be deadly: breathing stops, bleeding does not stop, or poison was ingested. Someone administering first aid must not delay when one of those three conditions is present. In standing for what's right, the criteria are not always so clear. Each situation must be weighed for the risk involved if you do take action as well as what is at risk if you *do not* take action. Here's where your own moral compass comes into use. Does your decision to take a stand or not have to do with saving lives? Does it have to do with holding true to your religious beliefs? Here's a real life example: a child is being beaten to death (God forbid). Calling the police or, if you are strong enough, stepping in to stop it, would of course be appropriate. A man once saw this happening during the Holocaust. But it was the "police" (Nazis) doing the murder. Had the witness (who survived to tell about it) stepped in, both he and the child would have been dead. The same man went on to save countless other lives in other ways as a partisan fighter, as well as by helping people to escape from Nazi territory.

Contrast this to fighting over a collect call rip-off of eight dollars that would take hours and hours of time to collect. Okay, so these examples are extreme. Within you lives your own scale of justice. Have it calibrated with good guidance from people you respect and trust.

It's a paradox: sometimes you have to fight for peace. It is kind of like cancer. Sometimes the solution is to fight to get the part out that is making you sick. Sometimes in this world, it is worth it to make sacrifices to keep the world just and safe. It is never fun to fight. But sometimes it is necessary. Avoiding a fight is the best when you can. When you have to, choose your battles carefully.

CALIBRATING YOUR MORAL COMPASS

When you're not sure which battles you should be fighting, it's a good idea to seek out spiritual or religious leaders who can offer guidance to keep you on track. Seeking guidance does not mean you stop thinking for yourself. This is not the time to let your common sense or your intuition go to sleep. There are people who would mislead you for their own personal gain of money, ego, or power. The place inside you that knows what is right and wrong, good and evil, also knows what kind of guidance you are willing to receive. You have to use your instincts, pay attention to the red flags. And always know that you have a connection to God, your Higher Power—or however you want to think of the Source of life—right *inside of you.* You have an instant connection whenever you will it. All you have to do is *want* to connect and the connection is there.

WALKING A SPIRITUAL PATH IN LIFE

I took a class once where the teacher asked: You walk into a store to buy a jacket and see a large rack filled with just the jacket you want. They are all the same manufacturer, same color, same cut, same price, same material. How do you know which one to buy?

Hmmm.

He went on to reveal: the one that fits. If you don't know which path is a fit for you, you may need to try some on to find out (study, explore your own roots, or even ask the Powers that Be for a hand).

Everything you have ever studied begins with accepting an idea. When we talk about a spiritual walk, what the heck does that mean? It means that there is more to this life than our physical selves. How do we know? When you get a haircut or change your clothes the essence of you does not change. Whether you are feeling good or feeling down, you are still you. When you understand or are confused, you are still you. When you were seven and when you will be seventy, you are you. The you that turns around when your name is called. The you that goes inside with feelings in your body that reflect what is going on in your mind and heart, the you that is living this life.

The first reality in the walk is understanding that you are more than your body, your feelings and thoughts; you are a soul. One way to consider it is that you are not a physical being having a spiritual experience, but rather a spiritual being having a physical experience. Don't be afraid to explore the spiritual side of yourself, give it expression, and let it be a guiding force in your life. That's what life is about.

BEWARE THE BLURRING OF RIGHT AND WRONG

It is a wonderful thing in our society that we strive to be tolerant of others' differences. But be careful not to lose your powers of discernment in your efforts at being non-judgmental. Judging means making distinctions. Judging others' souls is beyond our realm. Judging their actions—and reacting to them when necessary—is a skill that can keep you and the people you love safe.

There are those who would confuse you by blurring the lines between right and wrong, or good and evil, by feeding you some truth and some lies mixed up together. When we see the truth in what they say, we tend to give them credibility or believe the rest of the story. A little bit of truth is not truth.

> "There are two ways to slide easily through life:
> to believe everything or to doubt everything;
> both ways save us from thinking."
>
> –Alfred Korzybski

LIVE YOUR DREAMS

"Dream lofty dreams and as you dream,
so shall you become.
Your Vision is the promise of what you shall one day be."

–James Allen

We each have many dreams. Not the kind of dream you have at night when you are sleeping, and not the daydream fantasies that are not based in reality. I'm talking about the dreams that come from your heart's desires. You can tap into your heart and find out what your heart's desires really are.

- What is it that you love?
- How can you reveal your dreams?
- How can you make your heart's desire a real part of your life?
- What do you need to let go of to make room for what you want?

- How will you know when you have reached your goals?
- How will you celebrate and acknowledge when you are successfully living your dream?

IDENTIFY YOUR DREAMS

Even if you think you are crystal clear about what your dreams are, it is worth it to let your imagination soar with these exercises. You may surprise yourself with some ideas and you may strengthen or expand on what you already know is an important dream and heart's desire.

Exercise #1: Win the Lottery!

Make a list of all the things you'd do and buy if you won the super jackpot lotto. A really long list. All the toys, cars, houses, stuff, fun. Keep going until you have exhausted any ideas. Then keep listing more until you are done spending money and now you are spending your time exactly the way you want. There should be at least 101 things on your list. In addition to a great list of goals and dreams, we are looking for a "bottom line."

If you get as real as you can and push yourself past the surface, you'll also see that you can actually create at least the beginning of that desire for yourself right now! Once people get past the material things they want to *have,* it becomes more about what they want to *do* and *who they want to become.*

What do you love to do, really love to do?

You are not limited to one dream!

You can have a whole list of dreams.

What happens for a lot of people is that once they have imagined spending all the money they can, the desire to do something helpful arises. If you really worked this little exercise through, you may have found that too. It may look like a list of gifts you give people. Or it may be a large sum of money to a particular cause. Often as people fill themselves up with their real, true heart's desire, they find that making a difference is what matters most and would give their life great meaning. And you don't need to wait to do that. If you have ferreted out a piece like that, you can start to fill yourself up through the gifts of service you have to give (you can read the chapter "Lend a Hand" again).

Exercise #2: Treasure Map

Have some fun with this: Get a poster board (a regular piece of paper will also do). Color is good. Then go through magazines and cut out photos, words, phrases, etc., that represent one of your dreams. Arrange the photos on the page so they look good to you, then glue them down. This is yours and you don't have to show it to a soul if you don't want to. You can make as many as you want. It's a creative art project that gives you a chance to explore what you have going on and what you love. Some of the themes you might want to explore include:

- Sports and fitness
- Family
- Travel
- Relationships
- Work or career
- Finances

You can put this "treasure map" up so you can see it, or just tuck it away somewhere to have a look at some time later. It's good to have an image in your mind that helps you direct your thinking (and so your actions) towards your dreams. Positively imagining your dreams and goals as if they are already in the process of coming true gives them a power that should not be underestimated.

"No pessimist ever discovered the secrets of the stars,
or sailed to an uncharted land,
or opened a new heaven to the human spirit."

–Helen Keller

CLEAR THE WAY
Another element of going after your dreams is knowing what you have to let go of in order to get what you want. It's about potential versus actual. Potential is always so full of promise, but it never is yours. A body builder must let go of regular ice cream sundaes and French fries to get the desired body. To become a responsible parent one must let go of a degree of freedom and put the child first. To heal emotionally letting go of grudges is a key. You get the picture. Letting go of one thing—sacrificing—is part of the picture of getting something bigger, better, or more fulfilling. You have to let go of the old job to get the new one with more opportunity. Do you want someone who will make a commitment? Let go of the person who does not commit.

Scary? Sometimes it is. That's okay. There are plenty of people who have walked the road of risk and celebrate the freedom of having let go where they needed to. It's the in-between place that's scary, the place between letting go of what you don't want and actually getting what you do want. That's the place where you grow, and growth is the path to your dreams.

SET YOUR GOALS AND PRIORITIES
Once you have brainstormed about your dreams, it's time to turn them into concrete goals. Look at what you love to do: what about it do you love? Is there something you feel compelled to accomplish? If you have tapped into your heart's desires, you will find clues to what is important for you.

Maybe your goal is to discover *what* it is that *you* love. Everyone has different goals. Everyone is motivated by different things. Some people love sports, some love to talk, some love to design. Maybe your goals are basic, like the goal of getting out of debt or finishing school or getting fit.

While it is wonderful to dream, if we ever want to turn our dreams into action we have to get realistic about the fact that we can't do *everything* we want to do. If we want to move beyond the potential paralysis of becoming over-whelmed by our goals, we must learn to prioritize.

What is most important to you? Sometimes a priority is fulfilling a commitment you made, paying a bill, or completing a class. Sometimes a priority has to do with your moral obligations, like participating with your family. Sometimes there is a time frame within which things need to be done. It is helpful to set all of your "things to do" out in front of you in a list so you can see them side by side.

There is a story about a professor who placed a large glass jar in front of his students. The object was to fill the jar as full as he could make it. He began by placing large rocks into the jar. He questioned the students about the capacity of the jar to hold more. They all agreed it would not. So he pulled out some small rocks and dropped them between the big rocks into the jar. They filled in the spaces between the rocks until everyone agreed that the jar could hold no more. Next he poured in sand, which filled in all the small spaces. Everyone agreed once again the jar was now completely full, until the professor began to fill the rest of the container with water.

Had he begun with the sand, he would not have fit in the larger rocks (biggest, most important goals). Take what is most important to you—the largest rocks that you will want to fit into the jar of your life—and make sure that you get those in. The smaller, less important stuff will fit around the major goals.

Another facet to consider is that what is essential is often not pressing. It seems like it will always be there for you to come back to. The danger is that you can let the truly important things in your life fall by the wayside if you spend all your time on the things that appear to be time-sensitive but don't truly impact the quality of your life. Spending time with the people you love and who love you is so essential to a happy life. Some people take it for granted that those they love will always be there. There are no guarantees in life, so take care of what is most precious to you.

IDENTIFY THE STEPS

"Setting a goal is not the main thing.
It is deciding how you will go about achieving it
and staying with that plan."

–Tom Landry

Once you've written down all your hopes and dreams, and then chosen what is most significant, writing them in a place where you can review them will give them even more power. Like everything else, we begin with our ideas, but then those thoughts must be put into action. Writing them down is the first action step you can take to make your dreams into a reality. Once you write down the major stuff, next you can break each part down into the smaller steps you need to take to get to the final place you want to be.

How do you eat an elephant?

One bite at a time!

That's how to approach your dreams. We dream big but it is impossible to step into the life you dream of without effort, without taking the concrete steps. Your dreams for your life, like building a house or anything else, must be accomplished one piece at a time.

An important aspect of this is that if you take the small steps to get to your dream, you can enjoy the success for each small step all along the way. This helps to create a journey that is a celebration instead of a frustration. One small step at a time will get you there. One dish at a time cleans the kitchen. One deposit at a time creates a savings. One interview at a time gets the job.

PERSISTENCE

Persistence is the key once you have outlined what you want and what you need to do to achieve your goal. That means you don't give up whenever you reach a tough place or a challenge. It means that even though the steps you are taking are small, you persist. You keep taking the small steps, knowing each one is getting you closer to your goal. Marathon runners all talk about a "wall." It's not a real wall but a personal breakthrough point, when things feel toughest but you keep pushing your way through in order to accomplish the goal. For the runner it's finishing the marathon—a twenty-six-mile run! Before runners can even get to the marathon, they have to start out running a little each day, then a little more and so on until they are running the full-out marathon.

Earlier in the book was a list of people who, when going after their dreams, experienced defeat and rejection. But they persisted and their persistence paid off.

There is a great story about an enormous field of daffodils. Can you imagine it? A field of bright yellow flowers as far as your eye can see, standing tall and bright, vibrating with the sun's light. A sign stands at the edge of the field telling just how it got there. It was planted by one person. ONE BULB AT A TIME. You can plant your "Field of Dreams," one step at a time. You just have to keep stepping, keep moving in the direction of your dreams. Course correct when you need to. Persist.

If you need to adjust your timeline, that's okay. Just keep moving in the direction of your dreams. Ever hike a mountain? You think you're almost at the top and just as you go around the corner, you see you have further to go. Keep going because eventually, you will make it to the top of your mountain.

SAVE SOMETHING FOR THE NEXT DECADE

I was talking with a very enthusiastic friend one time about our dreams. She shared a conversation with me that she had with another friend's mother. She was blabbing away about all that she wanted to do when the woman interrupted her and said, "Honey, save something for the next decade." It doesn't mean not doing what you want, just doing things at a nice pace so you can enjoy the journey. You don't need to plant all the daffodils at the same time—one bulb at a time will get you that field of beauty. As you travel along life's paths, as your perspective changes, things will rise to the surface naturally.

Some things need to ripen at their own pace and some things you need to just jump into. I wish there was a formula I could share with you so that you'd know just what to do and when. Hey, I wish I had the formula for myself! But then, not always knowing is one of the delicious mysteries of this journey. The journey is a source of challenges, surprises, and delights, too. It is kind of like painting with water colors. You can control it to some degree, but the very nature of the medium means there will be surprises. You are co-creating. In life, part of the medium of your art is time.

> "Nothing in life just happens.
> You have to have the stamina
> to meet the obstacles and overcome them."
>
> –Golda Meir

CHANGES

Growing up, Letting Go, Moving On

"Change is not merely necessary to life. It *is* life."
–Alvin Toffler

Changes can be overwhelming. As you face a new stage in life, you are entering unknown territory. What will it be like for you? Will you be successful? Will you be okay? Change can be daunting (and scary) when you didn't plan for it. Even when change happens for the best of reasons—a graduation, a new job, marriage, a baby, a new house—it is still an effort to find the new balance. It takes effort and attention and maybe some risk. How do you approach change? Remember the riddle about eating an elephant, one bite at a time?

APPROACHING CHANGE
One breath at a time, one decision at a time, one hour, one day at a time. Choose the small increment that is bearable for you, then step forward. This is a time to listen to your

239

intuition. This may also be a time to ask for moral support and encouragement from friends and family.

There is an interesting thing about time—it keeps moving forward. Time can seem to move so slowly, when challenges are present. Other times, we want to grab the good times and never let go. Albert Einstein explains relativity: "When a man sits on a hot stove for two minutes and it seems like two hours, or when a man sits for two hours with a beautiful woman and it seems like two minutes, that is relativity!" In life, there will be challenges and good times. The seasons are guaranteed to change one to the other, summer into fall, winter into spring. When someone is experienced in something they are sometimes referred to as "seasoned." They know the ebb and flow, the rising and falling of time. One important key in successfully passing through each change is the way you hold yourself in relationship with others and, perhaps more importantly, the way you relate to yourself within any given situation.

REPLACE FEAR WITH EXCITEMENT
What are your perceptions? Redirect the same emotional energy which you named "fear" and give it a new job: "excitement." Take frustration and redirect it to gratitude. This is steering with your intention.

Some years ago a friend of mine lost a child to cystic fibrosis. It was not long after that loss that I found myself exhausted and one of my kids would not stop crying. I was feeling so frustrated and tired when this thought hit me like a ton of bricks: *oh, what she wouldn't give to be in my place and hear her son crying!* I can't tell you how it jolted me into gratitude that my problem was a crying kid! Gratitude is like a lifeline that can pull you out from wallowing and into a blessed paradise!

When you're facing changes and it feels scary, you may not want to hear about someone else's triumph over a difficult adversity. If that's where you are right now, take a minute to be tender with yourself. Do something nurturing: eat pizza or chocolate, burn a candle, call a friend, play some ball, take a bath, go to a movie, whatever does it for you. Then, get over it and grab onto the inspirational coat-tails that are before you. You can take some more time to rejuvenate and regenerate on the other side of the change.

Remember King Solomon's ring: "This, too, shall pass." The following famous poem (*Ecclesiastes 3:1-8*) was also written by King Solomon:

Everything has its season, and there is a time
    for everything under the heaven:
A time to be born and a time to die;
    a time to plant and a time to uproot the planted.
A time to kill and a time to heal;
    a time to wreck and a time to build.
A time to weep and a time to laugh;
    a time to wail and a time to dance.
A time to scatter stones and a time to gather stones;
    a time to embrace and a time to shun embraces.
A time to seek and a time to lose;
    a time to keep and a time to discard.
A time to rend and a time to mend;
    a time to be silent and a time to speak.
A time to love and a time to hate;
    a time for war and a time for peace.

WHEN PEOPLE AROUND YOU ARE CHANGING

Another aspect of change is when people you have spent a lot of time with seem to change. What then? Perhaps their change is a reflection to us that we need to make a change, too. Get stronger or better or smarter (or even get out of there). Perhaps the people around you haven't changed as much as you think and it is you that has changed. Thoreau said it well: "Things do not change; we change." There is an old saying that the more things change, the more they stay the same. No matter how high tech the world becomes, it will always come back to where you live within yourself. How you relate to yourself, how you perceive the issues that arise, and what you do. It will always come back to relationships—with yourself, others, God.

JUST DO IT

One moment flows into the next, yet we are constantly in the present. On top of that, the present keeps changing. So, how do we learn to let go and move on, how do we allow ourselves the freedom to be who we want to be and where we want to be?

It's kind of like breathing. You just do it. The more you think about it, the more self-conscious you become and the less natural it is. Still we need to let go of one breath and take in the next one. (Go ahead and take a deep breath; each breath is a blessing.)

While on a trip to Italy, I entered an unassuming building. Up the steps I went and entered the first in a series of rooms full of bones. I mean big rooms full of many piles of bones, skulls, and . . . bones. There was one whole skeleton who was dressed, and although hardly anyone I met in

Italy spoke English, this dead, grinning, bone guy had a sign in front of him in English. It said: *"Where you are, we once were. Where we are, you soon shall be."*

Interesting. It didn't take too long to sink in. A little creepy to think of myself all warm-blooded, someday going to be bones. A great opportunity for reflection, as I'm sure it was intended. Who we are during the thinking, pulsing, living moments is what counts in life.

We are always changing as we move through life. When we can take our life experiences—both positive and negative—and learn from them, then we are growing ahead. That growth, that life experience, gives you new points of view. Like climbing a mountain or a staircase. The more steps you take (toward growth and learning) the higher you get. The view changes because as you ascend, as you go higher, in addition to the different perspective, you can see more. When you are very young, you don't have a clue that you will ever change. By the time you are a teenager, you have a clue, but be careful because you may be under the illusion that you have reached the pinnacle, that final destination: "adulthood." If you are an adult who has paid attention and you understand the lesson that there is always more, then you certainly know that you never really arrive. It is all the journey.

"Sixty years ago I knew everything; now I know nothing. Education is a progressive discovery of our own ignorance."

–Will Durant

MOVING ON

You know that change happens. You know that letting go can take many forms. The moving on part is about knowing where and who you want to be, and then taking the steps in that direction. The way you move on is the relevant part. Not how fast you move, just that you're moving and that you're doing it in a way that is kind to you and others. Your willingness will give you the strength.

On Letting Go

Two Buddhist monks were walking when they came upon a river that they wanted to cross. At the edge of the river, they saw a woman who was afraid to cross the water. One of the monks picked her up, carried her across, and set her down on the opposite bank. She thanked him and they went their separate ways.

A few hours later, the second monk turned to the one who carried the woman and said, "I can't believe you carried that woman!" (A monk had made a vow of celibacy and would not touch a woman.) The first monk turned to the second and said, "I left her back at the river; you have been carrying her all this way."

THE GIFT OF TIME

It's your time. Take your time.

"Uncertainty and mystery are energies of life.
Don't let them scare you unduly, for they
keep boredom at bay and spark creativity."

–R. I. Fitzhenry

If time is a gift, how do you want to spend the gift of your
time? Keep asking yourself if what you are doing is the
way you want to spend the one resource you are given on
this earth. You can't control *how much* time you get, but
the *way* you live within the time you have is what matters.
Are you making your time count? There are many ways of
receiving this gift. One is by using yourself to improve your
small corner of the world in some small way. Even to grow
yourself, to overcome your personal obstacles, improves the

world. Are you connecting with people? Are you sharing your heart, your kindness, your deeds, your unique gifts? Are you living your dreams, following your heart (remember that small steps at a time get you there)? Do you let yourself enjoy the beauty of a moment or the world around you?

CONNECTING WITH PEOPLE
IN A DIFFERENT PLACE IN TIME

One of the challenges with our educational system is that it separates people from one another by age. It is illegal to separate people according to color or nationality, but for what seem to be developmental reasons, school systems have segregated people according to age. Old people forget what it is to be young. Young people don't know what a great resource old people are, and worse, are often uncomfortable talking with someone from another generation. And who cares about the really little kids? It is sad for us all. I hereby encourage you to go out and meet, and connect with, people of different ages. Maybe you can do some volunteer work with young kids. Take the time to really listen to their thoughts and ideas and imaginations. Maybe you can connect with some senior citizens.

Listen, people are people no matter what the age. Some are really wonderful to be around and some are so nasty or bitter (or wounded) that they push nearly everyone away. You might find that someone who appears a little grumpy is really just in need of some kind attention to open up the floodgates of friendship. Share a meal with someone from another decade and find out how things are different for them or even how they are the same. Share how things are for you now. It is so wondrous to connect in unexpected ways.

THE SECRETS OF TIME—TIME WILL REVEAL

Have you ever seen those large candles with the hidden treasures? You don't know where in the wax they are buried, but as the candle burns, the treasures are revealed and you can get to them. Time is like that, with treasures of knowledge and understanding and wisdom. *If you pay attention, time will reveal the things you don't understand about yourself or about someone who is close to you.*

A couple was married for sixty years. Whenever they would argue, the husband would walk out of the room. The wife would get mad and accuse the husband of running away from his problems. At a lecture she attended, the speaker talked of the dangers of anger and the way it disconnects you from yourself. When questioned about the best way to control anger in certain situations, the speaker said that if you can walk away until you have calmed down, that would be good. Suddenly, after sixty years, the woman realized that her husband had taken the high road by not yielding to his anger. Sometimes, especially when we give the benefit of the doubt to what we perceive as someone else's frailties, we just might discover, ten, or twenty, or sixty years down the road, that they made the lofty choice all along.

TIME IS A TREASURE, SO TREASURE YOUR TIME

At my aunt's funeral, some people got up to say a few words about her. When it was my uncle's turn, he spoke lovingly of her spirit. He wept while he spoke of their many years of marriage to each other. "No one told us how fast fifty-seven years would go." It's hard to imagine fifty-seven years as if they are the blink of an eye.

Sometimes we are climbing the mountain, sometimes we stop for a drink in the stream, sometimes we sleep. How much more meaningful a journey when we can notice all the gifts along the way.

TIME AS HEALER

Sometimes time is the healing factor. Time away from a situation can give you a chance to get some perspective. Sometimes we see things as worse than they are and time lets us lighten up. Time brings the perspective that lets us reconsider choices we have made and redirect our path with new and improved choices.

TAKE YOUR TIME

There are some things in life that, no matter how strong your intention is, no matter how much you do, simply need time. Strong muscles grow with each day's effort, a delicate flower opens in its season and in its own timing, a new baby will be born after it develops in the womb, friendship grows day by day and then year by year is strengthened by commitment, loyalty, and kindness. Do what you need to do, whether it's taking small steps in the direction you want to be, or taking a break. Take time for joy. Look for ways to spend time in joy on purpose. Remember, you see what you look for, so look for time to enjoy your life.

> "No great thing is created suddenly, any more than a bunch of grapes or a fig. If you tell me that you desire a fig, I answer you that there must be time. Let it first blossom, then bear fruit, then ripen."
> –Epictetus

A Final Word
THE WORLD IS YOUR OYSTER

"Far away there in the sunshine
are my highest aspirations.
I may not reach them,
but I can look up and see their beauty,
believe in them, and try to follow where they lead."

–Louisa May Alcott

I want to tell you about oysters. You know, the sea creatures that create the beautiful pearl. A pearl begins as an irritating grain of sand! It is an irritation to the animal and so it gets coated with a substance to make it smooth! That which began as an irritation becomes something precious. Your challenges become your gifts.

Have you ever seen a raw diamond? You might not recognize it. In order to reveal its beauty, it must be cut and polished—an abrasive process.

Okay, so we've established that this world holds all kinds of challenges. And you now know that you have choices about your attitude, actions, and perceptions. You know that you have to learn some things the hard way and you also know that not everything has to come hard.

The work involved in getting the pearl out of the oyster is in the harvesting. What it means when we say that the world is your oyster is that you need to get motivated to harvest the treasure. The treasure of life will look different to each person. Only you can determine what the real treasure is for yourself. You can ask others about the treasures they have found and look in those areas to see if they hold the same treasure for you. I've heard repeated often that connecting with loved ones is one of the most important things we can do and I'm inclined to agree. But hey, you'll discover what holds meaning for you.

Step forward into each new beginning with hope and promise. Find your courage to take one more step up to the best you and your truest dreams.

"Beware what you set your heart upon.
For surely it shall be yours."

–Ralph Waldo Emerson

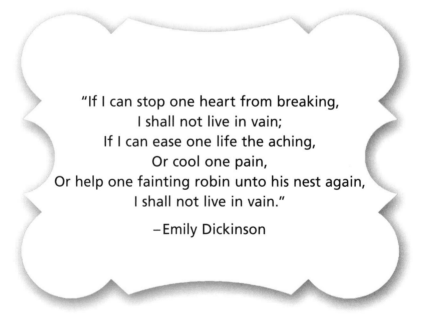

"If I can stop one heart from breaking,
I shall not live in vain;
If I can ease one life the aching,
Or cool one pain,
Or help one fainting robin unto his nest again,
I shall not live in vain."

–Emily Dickinson

RECOMMENDED READING AND BIBLIOGRAPHY

Below are books that I have found value in. I may not even agree with some of the things in some of these books, but I have found value nonetheless. As with everything I have written, you must discern for yourself if the information, teachings, etc., are a good fit for you. Keep in mind that just because something is in book form does not mean that what it contains is right. Judge books with the criteria of what you value.

Note: Please also see the recommended book lists at the end of the "Sexual Abuse" chapter (page 103) and the "Suicide" chapter (page 114).

Baker, Leigh, PsyD, *Protecting Your Children from Sexual Predators*.
New York: St. Martin's Press, 2002.
As the title implies, this book is written for parents. With the author's guidance, I used material from her book to help you, the reader. If you are a parent, this is a must-read.

Bass, Ellen, and Laura Davis. *Beginning to Heal: A First Book for Survivors of Child Sexual Abuse*. New York: HarperCollins Publishers, 1993.

Bean, Barbara, and Shari Bennett. *The Me Nobody Knows: A Guide for Teen Survivors*. New York: Jossey-Bass, 1993.
This is a down-to-earth book for survivors of sexual abuse. The authors "hold your hand" through the process of working through your feelings and deciding what steps to take next in your healing journey.

Benson, Peter L., PhD, Judy Galbraith, MA, and Pamela Espeland. *What Teens Need to Succeed: Proven, Practical Ways to Shape Your Own Future*. Minneapolis, MN: Free Spirit Publishing, 1998.
"*What Teens Need to Succeed* inspires and empowers teens to build their own assets. It invites readers to identify the assets they already have and the ones they need, clearly describes the forty assets identified as most essential, then gives hundreds of suggestions teens can use to develop the assets at home, at school, in the community, in the congregation, with friends, and with youth organizations."

DeBecker, Gavin. *The Gift of Fear: Survival Signals That Protect Us from Violence*. Boston, MA: Little, Brown, 1997.
Many insights to keeping safe and learning to trust yourself and your intuition.

Freeman, Tsvi, compiler. *Bringing Heaven Down to Earth: Meditations and Everyday Wisdom from the Teachings of the Rebbe, Menachem Schneerson.* Holbrook, MA: Adams Media Corp., 1999.
Words of wisdom from a contemporary sage on a whole spectrum of topics in "bite size" doses. (This is a Jewish book but appeals to a wide audience.)

Friedman, Manis. *Doesn't Anyone Blush Anymore? Reclaiming Intimacy, Modesty, and Sexuality.* San Francisco: Harper San Francisco, 1990.
Explore the issue of modesty, its value and place in today's world. Learn to honor yourself with guidance from this text.

Kuhn, Cynthia, Scott Swartzwelder, and Wilkie Wilson. *Buzzed: The Straight Facts about the Most Used and Abused Drugs from Alcohol to Ecstasy.* New York: W. W. Norton, 1998.
A non-judgmental "just the facts, ma'am" account of the full spectrum of drugs. If you like to be educated here is a great resource. As they say (and the title of another book by the same authors for people who care about kids), "Just Say Know."

Maltz, Wendy. *The Sexual Healing Journey: A Guide for Survivors of Sexual Abuse.* New York: Quill, 2001.
This is a great place to start. Ms. Maltz will guide and accompany you as you journey toward healing. Also listed in the book is an extensive section of resources.

Palatnik, Lori, and Bob Burg. *Gossip: Ten Pathways to Eliminate It from Your Life and Transform Your Soul.* Deerfield Beach, FL: Simcha Press, 2002.
The title says it all. A concise read, packed with practical information.

Shneidman, Edwin S. *The Suicidal Mind.* New York: Oxford University Press, 1996.
Although this is written with a pretty academic tone, there are some very deep insights to be found here.

Telushkin, Joseph. *Words That Hurt, Words That Heal: How to Choose Words Wisely and Well.* New York: W. Morrow and Co., 1996.
For a more in-depth discussion and insights on communication, gossip, etc.

ACKNOWLEDGMENTS

As I sit to write these pages I realize it is impossible to thank everyone who's influenced or been involved in supporting the birth of this book. There were many people I spoke with along the way who offered me support and encouragement—some whose names I'll never know but who smiled knowingly when I told them the title of the book and said they wish they'd had this book, too. Every smile cheered me onward.

I am blessed with many friends whose words of confirmation, affirmation, and feedback gave me the energy to keep going. The vision you held for me that this book would someday be a reality formed the golden bricks that lit my way and gave me a foundation: Annette and Haguy. Ruthie, Emily, Wendi, Bonnie, Sol and family, Sim and Phyllis, Cathy and Clint, Jeffrey and Shira, Susan and Brett, Zoshia, Madeleine, Sharen, and many others from beginning to middle to end.

Rabbi Yisroel Engel, you have always given more than asked for in gentle consideration and in friendship. My grateful thanks to Dar and Dale Emme and all the folks at The Yellow Ribbon Suicide Prevention Program.® To Ann Marie Akers, for sharing the knowledge you have on preventing drug abuse. To Dr. Leigh Baker, for sharing your knowledge on the painful subject of sexual abuse. Your help was given generously and on the wings of kindness. To Dr. Thomas Blass, who helped me accurately communicate about the important work of Milgram. To Pastor Dale Butler for his time and kind words. Each of you is a blessing in this world. And to the countless librarians who helped me with research. Thank you.

Eileen, Kent, Rachel: Your desire to read the pages I wrote is the reason I could even write one more word or one more page along the way. It is a privilege to know you and call you my friends.

To all the other "kids" who read and gave feedback anonymously, your ideas also helped shape this book.

To Leora, Ben, Chrissy, Ken, Kea, Kent, Max, Kirk, Gent, Eli, Whitney, Holly, Jules, Max, Tori, Elie, Eileen, Rachel: Thank you for showing up in this world and letting me love you. May each of you always know that your voice makes a difference in this world. Make each word count for the good.

To Kathi and Hobie and Liz for your patience, kindness, humor, and great ideas that contributed to getting this book complete. May the Force be with you always. Deanna, thanks for the best, most loving index ever.

Kezia, you fall into several categories all at once: editor, consultant, cheerleader, friend. My appreciation to you is more profound than words can tell. Your support through this project was way beyond anything I could ever have dreamed an editor could provide. This book would not be what it is without you. Your friendship is so dear to me. My gratitude is infinite.

My parents spent hours and hours of long-distance time listening to details just so I could hear my thoughts out loud. "You are the wind beneath my wings." I'm grateful I have a chance to say publicly how deeply I love you.

It is another amazing treasure to have in-laws who are so dear. Thanks to you for the hours of time you spent talking and dreaming with me. I love you, too!

Jeremiah and Avital: Without you in my life, I'm not sure this book could have come from me. Being your mother is the greatest honor this life could bring and it is only through the perspective of motherhood that I had the motivation to write this book.

Tyrone, thank you for supporting me in every way. Thank you for waking up in the middle of the night to talk when I whisper, "Are you awake?" Thank you for sustaining me through each step of this journey. Thank you for having faith in this book. Thank you for dreaming my dreams with me. And thank you for being with me through the challenging times, and smiling together at the joys of life. You lessen the pain of life and double the joy in the way you live each day.

I thank God for every blessing: for everyone mentioned above, for helping me find words when I need words, for silence when I need silence, and for the grace that gets me on my feet and keeps me going even when I fall on my face and have to learn things the hard way.

PERMISSIONS – GRATEFULLY ACKNOWLEDGED:

"Suicide Prevention" from the brochure by Yellow Ribbon Suicide Prevention Program®: www.yellowribbon.org.

"Sam's Sandwiches" and "Good, Bad, Who Knows?" from *Way of the Peaceful Warrior* by Dan Millman (New rev. ed. Tiburon, CA: H. J. Kramer; Novato, CA: New World Library, 2000) ©2000 by Dan Millman. Reprinted with permission of H. J. Kramer/New World Library, www.newworldlibrary.com.

Quotes from *Buzzed* by Cynthia Kuhn, Scott Swartzwelder, and Wilkie Wilson (New York: W.W. Norton, 1998) ©1998 by Cynthia Kuhn, Scott Swartzwelder, and Wilkie Wilson. Reprinted with permission of W.W. Norton & Company, Inc., New York, NY.

Excerpt from *The Dynamic Laws of Prosperity* by Catherine Ponder (Marina del Rey, CA: DeVorss, 1985) ©1962 by Catherine Ponder. Reprinted by permission. DeVorss Publications: www.devorss.com.

The five stages of abuse from *Protecting Your Children from Sexual Predators* by Leigh Baker, PsyD (New York: St. Martin's Press, 2002) ©2002 by Leigh Baker, PsyD. Summarized with permission of the author.

Excerpt from *Man's Search for Meaning* by Victor E. Frankl (Boston, MA: Beacon Press, 1992) ©1959, 1962, 1984. Reprinted by permission.

"Information about Sexual Abuse" excerpted from *The Sexual Healing Journey* by Wendy Maltz (New York: Quill, 2001). Reprinted by permission of the author.

Quotes from Rabbi Menachem Schneerson excerpted from *Bringing Heaven Down to Earth* compiled by Tzvi Freeman (Holbrook, MA: Adams Media Corp., 1999). Reprinted by permission of the compiler.

Excerpt from *The Thinking Jewish Teenager's Guide to Life* by Akiva Tatz (Southfield, MI: Targum Press; distributed by Feldheim Publishers, 1999) ©1999 by Akiva Tatz. Reprinted by permission of the author.

"An Autobiography in Five Short Chapters" from *There's a Hole in My Sidewalk* by Portia Nelson (Hillsboro, OR: Beyond Words Publishing, 1993) ©1993 by Portia Nelson. Reprinted by permission.

Excerpts from "Buying without a Test Drive" by Marc and Beth Firestone ©2001 by Marc and Beth Firestone. By permission of the authors.

Drawing on page 27 from *Mind Sights* (published 1990 by W.H. Freeman Company) used with permission of Roger N. Shepard.

Give the Gift of:

to your friends

to people you care for

to people you love

to the people who bug you!

Check your local bookstore or online at:
www.auntlaya.com

Keep in touch!

I'd love to hear from you!

Tell me:

- what you loved about this book

- how your life is going

- what else you want me to write about for you

- your success stories (Remember, success stories don't start successful. If you don't have success, it's not yet the end of the story!)

- lessons learned you want to share with others

Write me:

auntlaya@auntlaya.com

And visit the website:
www.auntlaya.com

LAYA SAUL spent an unusually long time in adolescence where she earned a Master's degree in "Life's Stupid Mistakes." She later went on to earn a Master's degree in Applied Psychology.

As a child she dreamt about helping kids. The older she gets, the older the group of people who fall into the "kid" category!

She hopes that every reader will be able to take something from her writing to live a richer life and be blessed.

Born in Los Angeles in 1956, Laya Saul is living her dreams with her family (husband, two kids, a dog and a cat).

Index

Expectations of others, 37–38. *See also* Parents; Relationships
    being realistic about, 38–39
    divorce and, 151
    friends and, 155, 158–159, 160

F
Failure, 63–67
Faith
    aloneness and, 118–120
    grief and, 81
    marriage and, 150
Family. *See also* Relationships
    parents, 137–143
    prevention of suicide and, 110, 111
    relationships and, 207–208
Fear, 27, 240–241
Feedback from others, 183–185, 186. *See* Coaching from others. *See also* Criticism
Feedback, giving to others, 186
Feng Shui, 127–128
Forgiveness, 213–215
    failure and, 65
    keeping friends and, 157
    regret and, 69–71
    relationships and, 130–132
    when to ask for, 215
    of yourself, 69–71
Frankl, Viktor, 46–49
Freedom, choice and, 46–49
Friends, 153–154, 160–161. *See also* Relationships
    false friends, 161–162
    keeping friends, 156–159
    longtime friends, 159–161
    making friends, 153–156
    peer pressure and, 85, 159, 162–164

G
Gawain, Shakti, 128–129
Genetic predispositions to addiction, alcohol use and, 87
GHB (date rape drug), 88. *See also* Drug use
The Gift of Fear (DeBecker), 13, 20
Gifts, 9–10, 29, 43–44
Giving of yourself, 217–220
GLBT (Gay, Lesbian, Bisexual, Transgender) youth, 111
Goals
    identifying the steps to, 234–235
    living your dreams and, 233–234
    marriage and, 149–152
    sex and, 192, 195
God, faith in. *See* Faith